Cover (left to right)
Left: **German battery in Longues-sur-Mer.**
Centre: **Omaha Beach, June 6th 1944.**
Right: **American cemetery in Colleville-sur-Mer.**

The beaches
of the D-Day landings

TEXT **Yves Lecouturier**
IMAGES **Isabelle Bournier**

Editions OUEST-FRANCE

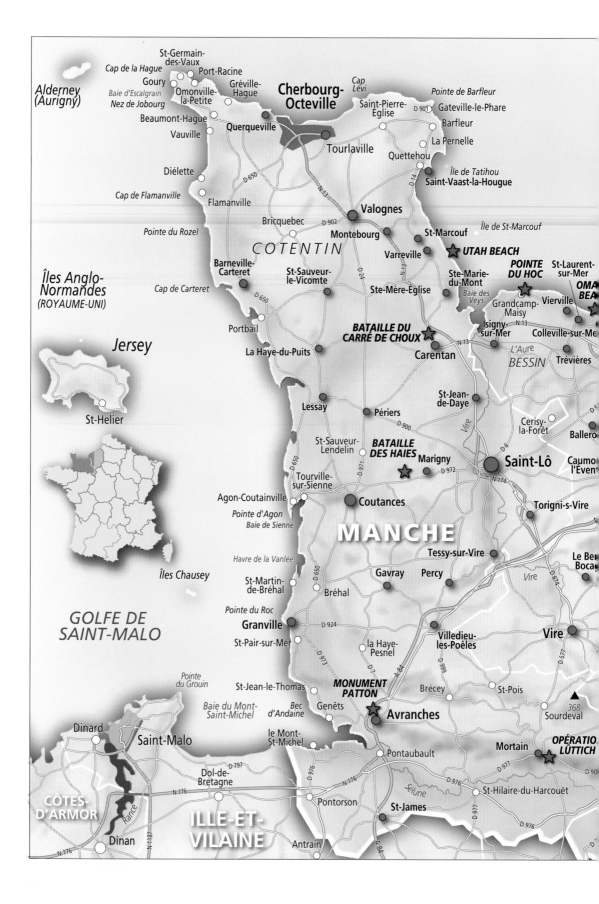

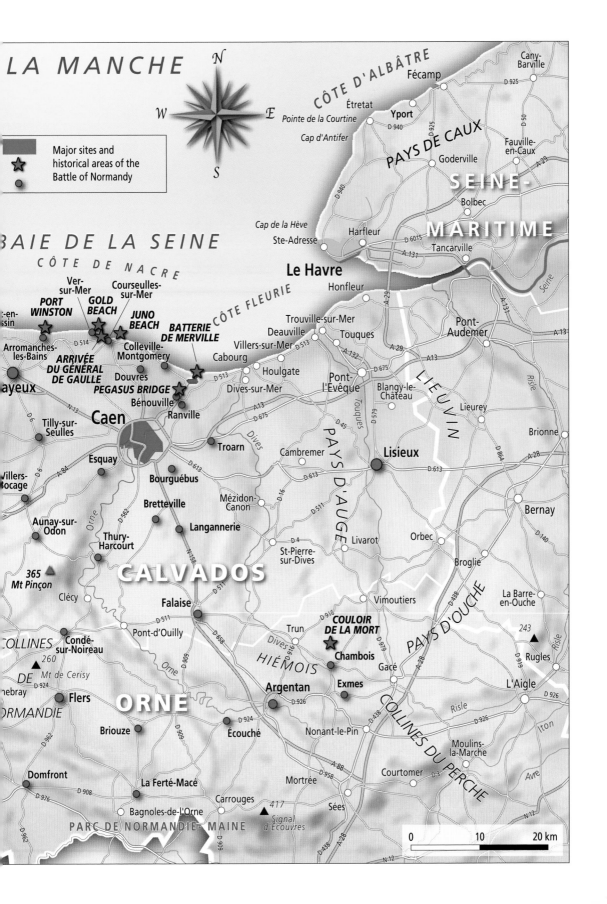

The preparations

In the summer of 1940, by creating a joint operations command, the British Prime Minister Winston Churchill demonstrated his determination to continue the fight and to take an active part in the liberation of Europe. Roosevelt and Churchill met a first time in Newfoundland in August 1941 and concluded the Atlantic Charter. A few days after the Japanese raid on Pearl Harbour in December 1941, Roosevelt and Churchill met again in order to work out a common strategy against the Axis powers and in particular against Germany. The Washington conference decided to create a joint general staff, the Combined Chiefs of Staff. On January 24th 1943, Roosevelt, Churchill, de Gaulle and General Giraud met in Casablanca with their chiefs of staff and decided to launch the landings on the north-western coast of Europe to defeat Germany: *"The war will continue until the complete and unconditional surrender of the foe."* This decision was accompanied by the creation

of a joint general staff or COSSAC: Chief of Staff of the Supreme Allied Commander. This task, assigned to the British General Frederick Morgan on March 12th 1943, comprised a vast amphibious operation to establish a bridgehead on the continent and to develop a decisive

Casablanca Conference, January 24th 1943.

attack aimed at Germany. British and American officers began to work together and on March 28th they met secretly in Scotland.

There were three methods of attack: Starkey, a diversion operation in 1943, Rankin, an attack ready at any moment if Germany collapsed, and Overlord, the landings operation of May 1944. The choice of the landing site favoured Normandy for meteorological and wind conditions, and also because the beaches were easily accessible and poorly defended. Since 1941, British commandos had worked mainly on the Calvados shores: Luc-sur-Mer on September 28th 1941, Saint-Aubin-sur-Mer during the night of September 27th to 28th of the same year and Saint-Laurent-sur-Mer during the night of January 17th to 18th 1942. These were mainly reconnaissance raids. On August 19th, Lord Louis Mountbatten, cousin of King George VI, in charge of the joint

operations, launched the 2nd Canadian Division on the German defences in Dieppe, but Operation Jubilee was a total failure; more than 4,300 men were killed, wounded or missing. Nonetheless, the Allies were able to learn from this for future landings on the Normandy coast. The same year, 1942, General George Marshall drew up the Round-Up plan for an Allied landing on the Channel beaches, but the British considered this to be premature. In May 1943, the Washington Trident conference adapted the main points of this plan which became Operation Overlord: it was approved in August at the Quebec Quadrant conference and planned for the month of May 1944. The COSSAC thus became an operational entity. Landing operations followed one after the other and were improved: Torch in North Africa on November 8th 1942, Husky in Sicily on July 10th

1943, and the Anzio landing in January 1944. By November 1943, four American divisions and three British divisions, all experienced, were moved from Italy and Africa. In December 1943, the Overlord supreme command (SHAEF: Supreme Headquarters Allied Expeditionary Forces) was entrusted to General Dwight Eisenhower. He appointed Sir Arthur Tedder as his second-in-command, Bertram Ramsay to supervise maritime operations and Trafford Leigh-Mallory for air operations, while Walter Bedell-Smith was made his chief of staff. Land forces were commanded jointly by Omar Bradley and Bernard Montgomery.

In January 1944, Eisenhower was given the following mission: *"You will enter the continent of Europe and, in conjunction with the other united nations, undertake operations aimed at the heart of Germany and the destruction of her armed forces."* In February 1944, he confided to Sir Bernard Montgomery that the plan for the landings needed to be revised: the front was widened from 25 to 50 miles, from the estuary of the river Orne (Calvados) to the Varreville dunes (Manche), and was to be attacked by five infantry divisions and three airborne divisions. At the same time, the date for the landing operations on the Côte d'Azur was changed to August 15th.

Operation Jubilee in Dieppe, August 19th 1942.

Since the failure of Operation Jubilee in the port of Dieppe there was no longer any question of attacking a port directly. The Allies therefore decided to adopt an idea of Winston Churchill to build an artificial port to disembark men, equipment and supplies: the port was to be prefabricated in England then convoyed across the Channel and assembled in situ. Twenty thousand workers were to manufacture the elements for the artificial port in a few months. Then there was the question of finding a solution to all the logistical problems posed by the landings, for example sending fuel across from the Isle of Wight to Cherbourg or the amphibious tanks. Ships were needed to transport soldiers and equipment. The whole of the south of England became one gigantic military camp firmly isolated from the surrounding population. The soldiers practised many exercises. For example, in May 1944, the Fabius exercise took place in Slapton Sands in Devon: the assault troops of the 1st and 2nd American Divisions carried out an amphibious landing as a rehearsal of what would happen during Operation Overlord. These exercises proved to be disastrous, with over 900 deaths.

The British paratroopers of the airborne forces repeated the taking of the Bénouville Bridge time and time again, until they knew the smallest details of the terrain.

There were three conditions needed to set the landing day – a high half-tide for the ships, a dawn assault and a full moon at night for

Fabius exercise, a rehearsal of Operation Overlord, Devon, May 1944.

the airborne troops – but these factors only coincided on a few days each month: in June 1944 the days were the 5th, 6th and 7th. On May 17th, Eisenhower set the date for Monday June 5th, with a possible delay to the Tuesday or Wednesday. The Allies prepared the landings down to the smallest detail since the liberation of Europe was at stake. If they were to succeed, they had to assert themselves quickly over the Germans through joint sea and air control. In 1943, American factories produced 30,000 tanks and 86,000 planes. All were sent to England on Liberty ships whereas the men, about 150,000 each month, travelled in steamers. At the beginning of spring, all the means of road and rail communication were systematically bombed in

Canadian propaganda poster.

American troops cross the Atlantic

Inspection of the Atlantic Wall defences.

absent from the landing beaches. In his book *The US Army Air Force in the Second World War*, John Flag writes: *"The Anglo-American air forces did more than just support the historic invasion of June 6th 1944; they made it possible".*

This airborne superiority was backed up by control of the seas after May 1943 when Admiral Doenitz decided to withdraw from the Atlantic Ocean. The battle of the Atlantic began in 1939, but became fiercer in 1940 when the Germans took the French ports. Until May 1943, German submarines ruled the ocean: between May and August, 97 submarines were sunk. On their side, the Allies mobilised everything which could float. On D-Day, each of the 187 Allied warships was given a very precise target. Apart from this mastery of the sea, the airspace was also under control, making it possible to fly in to bomb and pound Germany, but also France where the targets were the Atlantic Wall, radar stations, bridges and railway lines. In total, nearly 80,000 tons of bombs were dropped in the two months preceding the landings.

By the eve of June 6th, 1.7 million Americans had arrived. In total, the Allied armies comprised nearly 3 million soldiers spread over 39 divisions: 20 American, 14 British, 3 Canadian, 1 Polish and 1 French. A million men came from the Commonwealth. The rest comprised French, Belgian, Norwegian, Polish, Czech and Dutch formations.

The Allies tried to trick the Germans about their intentions by organising Operation Bodyguard, to make them think that landings would take place after the month of July and at a site which had not yet been decided. Among the hoaxes, the most remarkable was

order to isolate the north-west of France. From the month of April, all the coastal defences of the Atlantic Wall were targeted. In June 1944, Allied airborne forces (British Bomber Command and American Strategic Air Force) had more than 11,000 planes including 3,500 fighter planes and 5,000 bombers, while the Germans only had 500 planes. On D-Day, the Allied planes carried out almost 15,000 sorties whereas the Luftwaffe could only carry out 300! This meant that it was almost

Operation Fortitude. It consisted of convincing the Germans that the bridgehead for an Allied landing would be in the Pas-de-Calais. In order to do this, a ghost army was created from nothing, comprising decoys with for example decors in cardboard or rubber blow-up Jeeps and armoured vehicles. To complete the brainwashing, leaks were made to the press, but above all this phantom army was put under the command of George Patton. The spies of the Third Reich confirmed these dummy preparations. Despite several minor incidents, the great D-Day secret was kept until the end.

The French and Belgian resistants were and remained mobilised to find information about all the German plans, their positions and above all the movements of units. All this information, beginning with the theft of the Atlantic Wall map in May 1942 by a resistant, was a great help in preparing Operation Overlord. Apart from the

German sentry on the Atlantic Wall.

Beach obstacles known as "Czech hedgehogs".

presence of the 352nd German Infantry Division, which came to Bessin for manoeuvres, the Allies knew exactly where all the others were stationed.

The people of Normandy were not unaware that a landing could take place on their coasts. There were more and more evacuations in 1943 and 1944. In 1943, Cherbourg,

transformed into a fortress, saw the major part of its population evacuated to the south of the département. The Bessin coast and zone from Cabourg to Honfleur saw the same in May 1944. The idea of landings had entered the minds of the general public in Normandy. In January 1944, a report from French general intelligence noted that

"Grand Bunker" Museum, Ouistreham.

"*everyone is expecting important things to happen*". The landings were expected in the middle of March, and then in April, but in vain. The many German preparations and the intensified bombing led the French authorities to think that the landings were close. As a result, on April 25th 1944, the sub-prefect of Vire noted that "*the Anglo-American landings, considered to be imminent, are the order of the day*". Joseph Poirier witnessed this state of mind of many Normandy residents in the spring of 1944: "*We knew very well that deliverance was close, that liberation was coming, but we selfishly thought that the landings would take place somewhere else and that our region would be spared as it had been, miraculously, in 1940. Providence decided otherwise.*"

On the German side, the commander-in-chief of the Western Armies was Marshal von Rundstedt, but he had little room for manoeuvre and was thus uneasy. Besides this, his second-in-command, Erwin Rommel, had direct links with the Führer. Von Rundstedt did not believe that the Atlantic Wall could defend the European shores efficiently: he considered it as a "*gigantic bluff, less for the enemy, which knows its possibilities thanks to its agents and other information sources, than for the German population*". On September 29th 1942 the decision was taken to build, between then and the summer of 1943, 15 to 20 "pillbox" bunkers per mile along the coastline. In July 1943, only 8 out of the planned 15,000 had been built. Considering that the aim could not be achieved, Hitler focused his efforts on the Pas-de-Calais: 517,000 obstacles, among them 31,000 mines, were set there.

On the other hand, Rommel thought that he could play a decisive role, if only he had significant reinforcements. In a matter of a few months he built 4,000 constructions and planted thousands of wooden posts on the beaches together with cement blocks and a variety of obstacles. The dunes were mined and the exits from the beaches closed by barbed wire networks or anti-tank walls.

Thousands of acres of fields and pastures were flooded and "Rommel's asparagus" was planted as a defence against gliders. Despite these measures, the Germans seemed weakened because of their inferior air power: in spring 1944, only 500 planes were in flying condition. Von

Pillboxes in the Mont-Canisy battery.

🔲 **The Battery at Mont Canisy**
Tourist Information Centre, 32bis Avenue Michel d'Ornano, 14910 Blonville-sur-Mer, +33 (0)231879114
www.mont-canisy.org.
The Mont Canisy site, at the place known as "Le Grand Mont" in the town of Bénerville-sur-Mer, near Deauville, contains the restored remains of a major artillery position in the Atlantic Wall, overlooking the Seine Bay and the port of Le Havre. The numerous remains include around a hundred military structures of various types, including pillboxes and gun emplacements. Visitors can go more than 40 feet underground and explore 800 feet of tunnels and 25 underground barracks.

General Rommel on an inspection round on the Atlantic Wall.

Field Marshal Erwin Rommel (1891-1944)

He joined the army in 1910 and was wounded three times during the First World War. He was promoted to General in 1939, and then to Field Marshal in 1942. In June 1940, he crossed Normandy with the 7th Panzer. Hero of the Wehrmacht and appreciated by Hitler, he became famous at the head of the Afrika Korps in Libya, when he was given the name "Desert Fox". At the end of 1943, he inspected the Atlantic defences and was named head of the B group armies. On D-Day he returned to Germany, and then quickly came back to Normandy. On July 17th 1944, he was seriously wounded near Sainte-Foy-de-Montgomery when his car was strafed by two Allied aircraft. He advocated the establishment of a separate peace with the Allies, and supported the officers' plot against Hitler on July 20th. On October 14th 1944, while recovering from his injuries, he received the order to commit suicide, choosing to take poison rather than face a public trial. Four days later, he was given a state funeral.

Rundstedt had to defend about 3,000 miles of coastline with roughly 700,000 men. But he did not have the best units; on average they were relatively old and there were many *Osttruppen*, that is Soviet or Polish prisoners incorporated either willingly or unwillingly into the German army. In addition, Hitler remained convinced that an invasion could only take place in a port, whereas the Allies had abandoned this possibility since their setback at Dieppe. Despite this situation, the morale of certain troops was high, such as the 12th SS Panzerdivision "Hitlerjugend". But the morale of many German soldiers, convinced that the war was already lost, was very low.

Finally, Rommel and von Rundstedt quarrelled over strategy: the former wanted to stop the Allied landings on the beaches while the latter thought it preferable to let the Allies land and then mount a powerful counter-offensive using armoured divisions to force them back into the sea. Opposed to von Rundstedt, Rommel asked for armoured reserves to be based near the shore. Hitler took the decision and only allotted him three Panzerdivisions. Rommel was aware that any attempt to land in France had to be quashed immediately, since the risk for Germany was so great. On April 22nd 1944 he told his aide-de-camp: *"Believe me, Lang, the first twenty-four hours will be decisive... The fate of Germany will depend on it... For the Allies and for us, this will be the longest day".*

In order to succeed, the Allies spent months preparing a vast combined and mobilised operation to attack on June 5th, with 150,000 men, 20,000 vehicles, 11,000 planes and 7,000 ships. Every military action required follow-up logistics. It is one thing to establish a bridgehead, but to secure it is quite another. In the United States, Canada, Great Britain and the whole of the Commonwealth, everyone was ready to go and free Europe from the Nazi yoke. The many propaganda posters printed in the Allied countries are evidence of this.

Soldier from the Wehrmacht on the Atlantic Wall.

American poster: "Make every minute count".

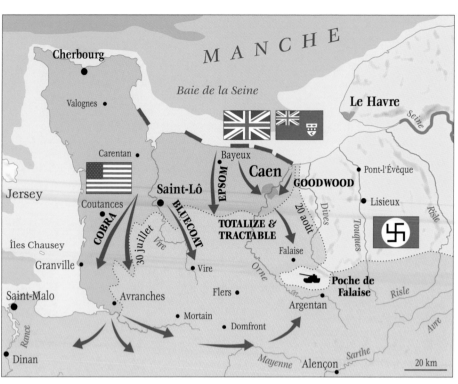

MANCHE

Baie de la Seine

Cherbourg

Valognes

Carentan

Saint-Lô

Coutances

COBRA

Jersey

Îles Chausey

Granville

Saint-Malo

Avranches

Mortain

Domfront

Dinan

Bayeux

Caen

EPSOM

GOODWOOD

Pont-l'Évêque

Le Havre

Lisieux

BLUECOAT

30 juillet

Vire

Vire

Flers

TOTALIZE & TRACTABLE

20 août

Falaise

Poche de Falaise

Argentan

Alençon

20 km

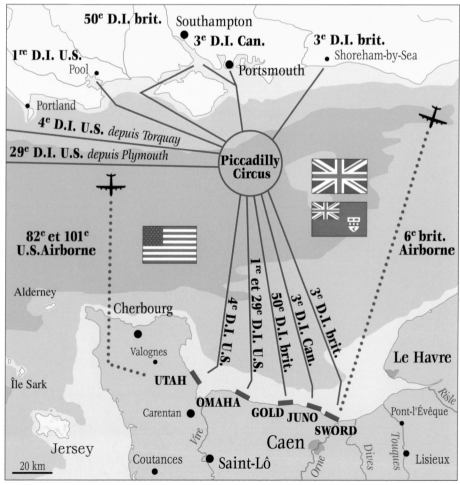

50e D.I. brit.

Southampton

3e D.I. Can.

3e D.I. brit.

1re D.I. U.S.

Pool

Portsmouth

Shoreham-by-Sea

Portland

4e D.I. U.S. depuis Torquay

29e D.I. U.S. depuis Plymouth

Piccadilly Circus

82e et 101e U.S. Airborne

6e brit. Airborne

Alderney

Cherbourg

1re et 29e D.I. U.S.

3e D.I. Can.

3e D.I. brit.

Le Havre

Valognes

4e D.I. U.S.

50e D.I. brit.

Île Sark

UTAH

Jersey

OMAHA

Carentan

GOLD

JUNO

SWORD

Pont-l'Évêque

Coutances

Saint-Lô

Caen

Lisieux

20 km

The landings of June 6th 1944

Two weeks before D-Day, the soldiers of the assault divisions were sent to camouflaged camps situated near the boarding zones. For these soldiers, any further contact with the local population or with their families was now cut. On June 1st, men and equipment took their places aboard the ships.

The climax was approaching, and this plunged the Allies into increasing anxiety. Whereas the month of May had been relatively pleasant, the first days of June were predicted to be more unsettled. The meteorological services noted that a depression was forming over Ireland and beginning to move south. On June 4th, the team of meteorologists led by Group Captain Stagg announced bad weather for the two following days with low cloud, a strong wind and rough seas: and these were the very days planned for the landings. The bad weather of June 5th made it especially difficult. So Eisenhower decided on a delay of at least twenty-four hours. This decision involved calling back the ships which were already getting under way. When the storm hit southern England,

Eisenhower congratulated himself on his prudence, but he remained worried about the following day. Luckily, Group Captain Stagg's meteorologists announced that it would be calmer on the morning of June 6th, and that this weather could last for thirty-six hours. The Supreme Commander of the Allied Forces therefore decided at 4.15 a.m. to launch the attack at dawn on June 6th. All the ships converged on the

Allied soldiers reading an information brochure about France.

Boarding of Canadian soldiers.

Final advice given by General Gale to his troops.

Isle of Wight during the day of June 5th to be ready to cross the Channel. The assembly point was named "Piccadilly Circus".

Like the people of Normandy, the Germans had been waiting for several months for a landing on the northwest shores of France. But the bad weather at the beginning of June convinced them that the Allied assault would be delayed for a certain time. Thus, on the morning of June 5th, Rommel left for Erlingen in Germany to see his family and to meet the Führer. At the same moment the generals of the 7th German Army went to Rennes for a meeting. During this time, the convoys were advancing across the Channel. The landing craft (LCTs, Landing Craft Tanks) crossed slowly at 4 to 5 knots. In order to keep up the illusion that Operation Fortitude was still in action, RAF bombers dropped little metallic sheets called "windows" in the skies over the Pas-de-Calais and Caux.

In the evening of the 5th, Eisenhower had visited the "screaming eagles", the paratroopers of the 101st US Airborne Division. He said to one of them *"Good luck for tonight, soldier"*, knowing full well that the first steps the Allied soldiers took on the Normandy beaches would be tragic.

Beginning at 9.00 p.m., the English radio began to churn out a series of messages aimed at the French Resistance to prepare the ground for Operation Overlord. *"The dice are on the mat"* and *"The long sobs of the violins of autumn wound my heart with a monotonous languor"* informed the resistants that D-Day was for the next day. The Germans knew the significance of the verses of Verlaine, but the information was not transmitted efficiently. On June 6th, Eisenhower addressed all the soldiers, aviators and sailors before they attacked the Normandy coasts: *"We can only accept total victory. Good luck to everyone and we implore the blessing of God Almighty for this great and noble enterprise".* After midnight, the 6th British Division under General Richard Gale launched its gliders to the north-east of Caen while the American paratroopers were dropped over Sainte-Mère-Eglise: Overlord had begun. These parachute drops were at the two ends of the landing shore in order to protect the assault from the sea on the beaches.

Each army corps had its mission to operate in a well-defined geographical sector with a precise task. Thanks to the many aerial photographs and the information transmitted by the French resistants, the Allies were

Eisenhower giving his final recommendations to the American paratroopers of the 101st Airborne. June 5th in the evening.

LES ARMEES ALLIEES DEBARQUENT

Allied leaflet dropped by aircraft on June 6th. On the back, General Eisenhower addresses the inhabitants of the occupied countries.

Portable MK2 transmitter station used by members of the Resistance to communicate with London.

well acquainted with the terrain they were entering. Therefore, on June 6th, just after midnight, the British paratroopers were the first to go into action north-east of Caen. Their mission was to take the Ranville and Bénouville bridges intact, at that time the only passing points over the river Orne and the canal linking Caen to the sea. The attack, rehearsed several times on an exact replica, was expertly led by Major

Howard. One cannot say the same for the American paratroopers dropped on Sainte-Mère-Eglise and scattered in the marshes in the middle of the Manche département: the swamps could not be detected by aerial photos. These first assaults backed up by general bombing of all their positions shook the Germans who still could not believe in a large-scale landing. These bombings destroyed 74 of the 92 German radar stations in Normandy. By applying the "violet" plan, the Normandy resistants were able to mix up communications: for example, the telephone cable from Cherbourg to Rennes, passing through Saint-Lô, was cut at Pontaubault by members of the PTT (post office) resistance network. Information did pass, but not enough to convince the German general staff that D-Day had come. Besides this, after listening to Wagner's music on the evening of the 5th, Adolf Hitler went to sleep and there was no question of waking him up!

At dawn on Tuesday June 6th 1944, an immense armada of 7,000 ships of all types was closing in on the shores of the départements of Manche and Calvados. On board were more than 300,000 men who had crossed the Channel through furious seas, many of them seasick. But despite this they were ready to land. For their part, planes and warships dropped thousands of tons of bombs on the Atlantic Wall. The weather on that morning of June 6th was grey over the beaches of Calvados and Manche. As far as the Allied soldiers were concerned, they only knew them by five code-names:
— **Sword Beach**, between Ouistreham and Lion-sur-Mer, assigned to the British 3rd Division under General Rennie;
— **Juno Beach**, between Luc-sur-Mer and Graye-sur-Mer, assigned to

the Canadian 3rd Infantry Division under General Keller;

— **Gold Beach**, between Graye-sur-Mer and Arromanches-les-Bains, assigned to the British 50th Infantry Division under General Graham;

— **Omaha Beach**, between Colleville-sur-Mer and Vierville-sur-Mer, assigned to the American 5th Army Corps of General Gerow, including the "Big Red One" of General Huebner;

— **Utah Beach**, on the eastern coast of the Cotentin peninsula, assigned to the American 7th Army Corps of General Collins, including the American 4th Infantry Division of General Barton.

The Americans landed at 6.30 a.m. at Omaha and Utah while at 7.30 a.m. the Commonwealth troops reached Sword, Juno and Gold beaches. At 6.30 a.m. Radio Berlin announced the landings. In its morning edition, the headline of the *New York Times* read "*The Allies have landed in France*". The great invasion was under way. General de Gaulle spoke on the BBC in the afternoon: "*The final battle has begun*". Hitler was informed at about 10 o'clock on June 6th that the landings were taking place on the Normandy beaches. He hardly seemed surprised but considered that it was only a diversion and that a much more powerful attack would take place in the Pas-de-Calais. Therefore, he refused to move more than two armoured units to the west, the Panzer Lehr and the 12th SS Panzerdivision "Hitlerjugend".

The landing operations continued throughout the day of June 6th, either without great difficulty as at Utah Beach, or with considerable loss of life as at Omaha Beach. By the evening, the Allied armies were well established on the coast of Lower Normandy. Most of the German defences and batteries had been neutralised. Over 150,000 men

and 20,000 vehicles had landed. In just a few hours, the Allied soldiers managed to penetrate several miles inland. Not all the aims had been achieved, but the five landing beaches were well held. The counter-attack of the 21st Panzerdivision on the Périers ridge had been contained by the British. But the advance of the Allied armies turned out to be more difficult than expected, for example in Caen, which had to be abandoned very quickly and was only fully liberated on July 19th, more than a month later. German resistance proved to be fiercer than expected,

American soldiers returning to their ship.

VICTORY OF THE ALLIES
IS ASSURED

resisted every inch of the way". The movement of the German reserves towards Normandy was delayed by the action of French resistants: thus the 2nd SS Panzerdivision "Das Reich", commanded by General Lammerding, put on alert in the evening of June 6th, only reached the south of Caen on June 28th! Even if Hitler demanded that *"each man must fight and die at his post"*, Rommel was much more pessimistic six days after the landings: *"The enemy is reinforced by the protection of greatly superior air power. Our aviation and our navy are incapable of providing adequate opposition. The enemy is reinforced much faster than our reserves arrive... Our position is extremely difficult: the foe prevents our making any movements during the day while itself it reorganises its own forces quite freely, even by air. The enemy has total control in the air over the combat zone and up to 60 miles inland."*

despite a relative absence of command. As Jean Compagnon emphasises, *"they used the terrain well, fired accurately, reassembled quickly and*

The days following June 6th saw an increasing number of bridgeheads being established, and by the evening of June 12th there were 16 Allied divisions present comprising more than 320,000 men accompanied by 54,000 vehicles and over 100,000 tons of equipment and supplies. This enabled the Allies to consolidate their positions in the following weeks before breaking through the German defences. The Allied superiority in the air was strengthened by the building of airstrips beginning on June 9th.

The battles for the liberation of Normandy, an essential prelude to the liberation of Europe, were costly in terms of both loss of life and heavy destruction. Cities, towns and villages collapsed under the bombing. The Battle of Normandy ended in the Falaise-Chambois Pocket where the troops of the Third Reich were surrounded and then defeated on August 21st 1944. This meant that the route to Paris and towards the east of France was now open, but it had taken two and a half months instead of the estimated three weeks.

These days, the beaches of Calvados and Manche receive many tourists each year, but each of their steps is marked by the memory of the biggest combined landing operation of all time. Each beach is a place of memory where those who pass by are asked to remember that thousands of men came here and died for the sake of freedom.

American soldiers land at Omaha Beach.

The British airborne sector

Twenty minutes after midnight, the British paratroopers and commandos launched an attack on the sector located immediately to the east of the river Orne. They were carrying out the mission planned by General Richard Gale, commander of the 6th Airborne Division: *"Take and hold the bridges on the Caen canal and on the Orne at Bénouville and Ranville... It is important for future operations that the bridges be taken intact."* This assault was intended to allow the British 3rd Infantry Division landing at Sword Beach to reach Caen rapidly. The task of the 6th Airborne Division was to occupy the sector between the rivers Orne and Dives north of the Colombelles-Sannerville-Troarn road and to launch attacks in order to delay the movement of the German reserves advancing from the east and the south-east. The parachute drops were not all successful, and some were scattered in flooded marshland shrouded in damp fog. Eighty-four Canadian paratroopers were taken prisoner as a result.

General Richard Gale, commander of the 6th British Airborne Division.

Bénouville and Ranville

Twenty minutes after midnight, Operation Tonga was launched: it was the first of a long series of operations within the framework of the Overlord plan. Three plywood Horsa gliders, which had been towed from England at 6,500 feet by Stirlings or Halifaxes, and each carrying 30 men from the 2nd Battalion Oxfordshire and Buckinghamshire Light Infantry integrated into the 6th Airborne,

landed on the narrow strip of land separating the canal from the river Orne, less than 50 yards from the Bénouville swing-bridge. They made up the Airborne D Company and were led by Major John Howard. In the lead glider, everyone was loudly singing the tunes sung several months before during training. At the moment they hit the ground at nearly 100 mph, the soldiers were holding each others' arms. The glid-er stopped only a few yards from the bridge. Willy Parr, a 22-year old English soldier, remembers: *"The pilot landed about twenty yards from the bridge. It was incredible!"* The Glider Pilots belonged to the army and had been trained specially for precision landings.

The two German guards were not aware of anything and were taken completely by surprise. The bridge was taken in ten minutes: this was

Bénouville bridge. In the background, the photo shows the gliders that landed at the foot of the bridge during the night of June 5th to 6th.

the first victorious exploit of D-Day. Major Howard set up his headquarters in a little village café and dance hall belonging to the Gondrée family.

Major Howard's men resisted all the German counter-attacks and held the bridge until the arrival of reinforcements, who were only two-and-a-half minutes late! These days this bridge is known as Pegasus Bridge in memory of the British airborne troops whose emblem was Pegasus.

At 1.30 p.m. on June 6th, No. 4 Commando led by Lieutenant-Colonel Dawson, which had landed six hours earlier on Sword Beach, crossed the bridge to join Major

Café Gondrée, Bénouville.

Pegasus Memorial

Avenue Major Howard,
14860 Ranville, +33 (0)231781944
www.memorial-pegasus.org
The Pegasus Memorial was built in the year 2000 at the initiative of the D-Day Commemoration Committee. It is dedicated to the missions carried out by the men of the British 6th Airborne Division during the Battle of Normandy. The story of these British soldiers is told through historical objects, documents and photos. Bénouville bridge, built in 1871 by Gustave Eiffel and renamed Pegasus Bridge on June 26th 1944, is on display in the park, together with a Bailey bridge and, since 2004, a life-size replica of a Horsa glider.

Pegasus Memorial.

Howard's men. Brigadier S. F. Lord Lovat, commander of the 1st Special Service Brigade, was followed by his personal "piper" Bill Millin, playing *Blue bonnets over the border*. At the same time the Ranville bridge was taken and resolutely defended, the paratroopers pushing back eight German counter-attacks. This conquest was announced as "ham and jam" by the BBC. In November 1993, Pegasus Bridge was dismantled and replaced by another better adapted to modern traffic conditions. A sound and light show is organised there every summer.

Taking these two bridges was the first Allied victory of the Battle of Normandy. It quickly led to the liberation of Bénouville and its town hall, the first to be liberated in mainland France.

The village of Ranville was liberated at 2.30 a.m. by the 13th Lancashire Parachute Battalion. The British soldiers assembled around the old mill and attacked the German garrison in Ranville. This was the first village in metropolitan France to be liberated. An hour

John Howard (1912-1999)
John Howard joined the army in 1932 and was assigned to the airborne forces; he specialised in taking bridges and therefore was put in command of the attack on Bénouville bridge: he became part of the legend of Pegasus Bridge. Seriously hurt in a road accident in Britain in November 1944, he had to leave the army and ended up as a government employee.

John Howard.

later, General Gale, after his trip on the Horsa No. 70 glider, set up his headquarters in lower Ranville: his statue can be seen today on June 6th Square. During the day of the 6th, the paratroopers had to push back two German counter-attacks. There is a cemetery next to the neo-Gothic church where 2,162 British paratroopers and commandos are buried. These include Lieutenant Dan Brotheridge, the first to be

Bénouville bridge, renamed "Pegasus Bridge", on display in the museum grounds.

Top: **British cemetery in Ranville.**

killed in the Battle of Normandy at the approach to the Bénouville bridge. There are also 322 German graves and 5 French graves in this cemetery. Opposite, there is a plaque on the old mill in memory of the Belgian brigade commanded by Jean Piron. The Pegasus Memorial in Ranville is dedicated to the British airborne troops.

Merville

These days, walking along the banks from Merville point to the mouth of the river Orne is very pleasant. Here, the sea goes out very far and opens up vast sandbanks. In the dunes there are still the remains of one of the three redoubts built in 1770 to defend the Orne estuary. South of the town, one-and-a-half miles from the shore, two blockhouses of a German battery defended by 130 soldiers still stand. Four concrete shelters hold four 100 mm guns with a 5-mile range. This battery, aimed at the Orne estuary, was considered to be the most important target in the region after the Bénouville and Ranville bridges. The battery was defended by anti-aircraft guns and searchlights, and also included an observation bunker. Seven hundred and fifty paratroopers from the 9th Battalion of the 6th Airborne Division commanded by Lieutenant-Colonel Terence B. N. Otway had trained rigorously for more than two months. They were equipped with the latest techniques. On June 6th, the paratroopers landed at about one o'clock in the morning, but only two gliders, including that of Otway, ended up in the right place; most of them were scattered around the battery. In an hour-and-a-half, Otway managed to assemble 150 men and decided to attack. At 4.45 a.m., having lost half of his soldiers, Otway

Top: **British cemetery in Ranville.**

Centre: **German graves in Ranville cemetery.**
Bottom: **Dan Brotheridge memorial stone.**

▣ Merville Battery Museum

Place du 9^e-Bataillon, 14810 Merville-Franceville,
+33 (0)231914753

www.batterie-merville.com

This museum tells the story of the battles fought by the British 9th Parachute Battalion under Lieutenant-Colonel Terence Otway to take the battery during the night of June 5th to 6th 1944. The vast site is run by a Franco-British Association, and contains around ten blockhouses, in particular four pillboxes (or casemates), a restored firing chamber and documents showing how the battery was organised. The daily life of the gunners is recreated in casemate no. 1 with sounds, lights and smells. Since 2008, a Dakota 43 plane has also been on display for visitors.

Top: **Pillbox in the Merville battery.**
Centre: **British Cromwell tank, Bénouville.**
Bottom: **Dakota 43 on display at the site of the Merville battery.**

Horsa glider taking off.

launched a rocket signalling "objective accomplished". This was only half an hour before bombardments started up again from the *Arethusa* cruiser out at sea. Otway and his men found nothing but old Czech guns. The German garrison was destroyed: out of 200 men, 178 were dead or unfit to fight. The spot was fought over repeatedly by the British and the Germans, and the battery changed hands seven times

Bottom left: **Paratroopers from the 6th Airborne Division.**
Bottom right: **Lieutenant-Colonel Terence Otway, Merville.**

Fusiliers Marins Commandos assigned to the British No. 4 Commando, led by Lieutenant-Commander Philippe Kieffer, landed here. Most of them, mainly Bretons, had joined de Gaulle in 1940. They had trained hard in Scotland, at Achnacarry camp. This was the only French unit involved on D-Day. It was integrated into the 1st Brigade commanded by Lord Lovat. Thirty were put out of action almost immediately after the landing. The others continued towards Riva-Bella by the Lion-sur-Mer road so as to take the enemy from behind. The aim was to capture the casino which had been transformed into a small fort by the German defence. The old casino in the Anglo-Normand style was demolished in 1942 to be rebuilt as a stronghold with two 20 mm guns on the roof. A veteran of the 1914-18 war from Ouistreham guided the green berets across the town so that they could take the casino from the rear. However, tanks had to be brought into action for the mission to succeed.

A villa, located these days behind the monument to No. 4 Commando, served as rallying point for the commandos and as a forward medical post. Access to this beach was defended by fortifications equipped with a battery of six 155 mm guns, machine guns and mines: nearly half the green berets perished here. A steel dome sheltering the machine guns overlooks the beach.

Slightly apart from the coast road stands the Grand Bunker, a concrete tower 55 feet high. This building has five floors, and the highest has a wide slit for observation and for setting up a telemeter for adjusting the range of fire. An Atlantic Wall Museum is to be found here now: on the 5th floor, it is possible to look at

Memorial stone in Colleville-Montgomery.

Remains of German defences on Ouistreham beach.

 Atlantic Wall Museum

Avenue du 6 Juin, 14150 Ouistreham, +33 (0)231972869
www.musee-grand-bunker.com
This museum, housed in a 56 ft high concrete bunker that contained a German firing post and military headquarters, uses costumed figures and a range of equipment and objects to recreate the original conditions over the bunker's five floors. One room is devoted to the history of the Atlantic Wall, with previously unseen photos and documents. The top floor contains a German range finder which offers stunning views over a 25-mile radius of the Seine Bay.

Philippe Kieffer.

Emblem of No. 4 Commando.

Philippe Kieffer (1890-1962)

This lieutenant-commander, an escapee from Dunkirk, joined General de Gaulle in London in 1940. First of all he was assigned to the battleship *Courbet* and then, in 1942, he joined the British commandos. With several Frenchmen he formed the *1er Bataillon de Fusiliers Marins* under the command of Lord Lovat. He took part in Operation Jubilee against Dieppe in August 1942. His commando was the only French unit to land on June 6th. He wrote: "*At this precise moment, the earth and the sea seemed lifted up in a crash of thunder: mortar bombs, the whistling of artillery shells, the terrible yapping of machine guns; everything seemed concentrated on us.*" Later he tried to enter politics in Calvados: he was elected departmental councillor for Isigny in 1945, but was beaten in the general elections of 1946.

Memorial stone in tribute to Commander Kieffer.

Bottom: **No. 4 Commando Museum, Ouistreham.**

No. 4 Commando Museum
Place Alfred Thomas, 14150 Ouistreham, +33 (0)231966310
www.musee-4commando.org
On June 6th 1944, 177 French green berets under Commander Kieffer, integrated into British No. 4 Commando, landed at Sword Beach. This museum pays tribute to the commitment of these commandos through a range of memorabilia and documents. Léon Gautier, one of the last surviving green berets, comes to the museum from time to time to describe his experiences. A film portrays the French commandos capturing the casino.

the horizon through the telemeter and to see as far as 28 miles over a 180° range.

Not far from here, another museum, the No. 4 Commando Museum, recounts the action of the green berets under Philippe Kieffer.

Near the embarkation port for England stands a lighthouse monument. Ouistreham was liberated at 1 o'clock in the afternoon, but only 60 French commandos were still fit to fight. A monument in the shape of a flame, on Boulevard Aristide-Briand, recalls the sacrifice of the Free French on June 6th 1944. This work in aluminium, on top of a dome, is by Yvonne Guégan, an artist from Caen.

Near it, a memorial stone pays tribute to Philippe Kieffer.

The 11th- and 12th-century Norman church has a stained glass window offered by the Commando Association in honour of the action of the marine commandos on D-Day. The picture is by the painter

Raymond Bradley; at the base is the inscription: "*1939-1945. To the glory of God.*"

Hermanville-sur-Mer

The landing took place in the narrow sector between the Hermanville breach and Lion-sur-Mer. Despite the swell of the tide, the British managed to disembark 21 of their 25 amphibious tanks. The town was liberated around 10 o'clock in the morning by the South Lancashire Regiment. At sea, at just over a mile from this breach, flying the flag of the Free French, the cross of Lorraine, the *Gustave-Courbet* battleship was scuttled to act as a "blockship", thus forming a breakwater with six cargoes and two other warships. The coast road is now named after Admiral Wietzel, the last captain of the *Gustave-Courbet;* the admiral laid his battleship flag in the

Landing in Hermanville-sur-Mer.

Monument commemorating the landings erected on a German armoured turret.

town hall. The chapel has stained-glass windows commemorating the landing. Near an 18th-century manor, a cemetery was created to house 986 graves of British and French commandos.

On the village square, the visitor can see the well of the Saint-Pierre pond, cited by the British army for having supplied 7 million litres of water from June 6th at 7 o'clock in the evening until July 1st. Thirty taps are to be seen along the wall of the presbytery. In the neighbouring woods, the British set up twelve field hospitals.

Lion-sur-Mer

While he was inspecting the Atlantic Wall, Marshal Rommel was photographed in the company of his officers at the end of the Rue des Bains in front of a half-timbered villa. This commune was liberated on June 7th by the 41st Royal Marine Commando after fierce fighting and the Haut-Lion castle was taken after two hours' resistance. There is a monument next to a tank in memory of the action of the British soldiers.

Luc-sur-Mer

At low tide the sea uncovers a beach of sand and pebbles where one can collect great quantities of seaweed. The beach is edged by a long promenade and a cliff pitted with notches eroded by the sea which are called "confessionals". This beach had been visited by a British commando on September 28th 1941: the aim of this raid was to take sand samples and to analyse them. There is a memorial stone in memory of this action with an invitation to the visitor: "*Passer-by, stop and meditate.*" This memorial stone also commemorates the arrival of Lord Lovat's commandos and the 4th Special Service Brigade of Brigadier Leicester. Luc-sur-Mer was liberated on June 7th after a short encounter in the Petit-Enfer led by the 46th Royal Marine Commando.

However, the British troops did not advance fast enough, which enabled General Wilhelm Richter, commander of the 716th German Infantry Division, to move his defences north of Caen, into the

Memorial stone in Luc-sur-Mer.

Lébisey woods. This installation prevented Caen being taken in the evening of June 6th, as planned by Operation Overlord. However, General Rennie managed to link up with the elements of the 6th Airborne Division which had arrived early on June 6th from the other bank of the river Orne.

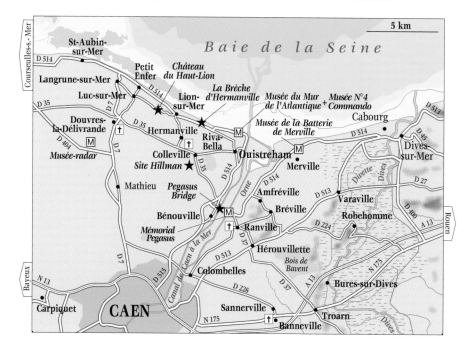

Juno Beach

Landing in Bernières-sur-Mer, June 6th 1944.

The Canadian 3rd Infantry Division under Major General R. F. L. Keller, comprising 15,000 Canadians and 9,000 British troops, set foot on the beaches of Vaux at Saint-Aubin-sur-Mer on June 6th just before 8 o'clock in the morning, heavy seas having delayed them by twenty minutes. The mission was to advance on Caen and take its airport, Carpiquet.

These Canadian soldiers wanted their revenge after Dieppe, but the beaches of this sector were defended by pillboxes sheltering cannons and machine guns. About 14,000 mines had been set as well as other obstacles of all kinds. Nonetheless, the German defensive system was not very powerful on this part of the shore. In fact, the Kriegsmarine

Top: **General Keller in Bernières-sur-Mer.**
Bottom: **Canadian troops preparing to land.**

specialists had decided that the rocks of Calvados should prevent any landing there. On June 6th, the leading Montreal daily newspaper, *La Presse*, saluted this Canadian landing with a front page headline *"The Canadians see Normandy again"*.

Beach defence,
Saint-Aubin-sur-Mer.

Langrune-sur-Mer

This town is known for its fine sandy beach bordered by a promenade, and has a 13th-century church with a lantern tower topped by an elegant spire with pinnacle turrets. Most of the villas overlooking the seafront were fortified by the Germans. A group of houses was transformed into a stronghold and equipped with 50 mm anti-tank cannons. The defences resisted during the whole of June 6th despite naval bombardments and fire from two light Centaur tanks. The commune was liberated on June 7th at about

Memorial stone in tribute to the 48th Royal Marine Commando, Saint-Aubin-sur-Mer.

3.30 p.m. after fierce fighting, the soldiers of No. 48 Commando led by Lieutenant-Colonel Moulton having to fight house by house, opening breaches in the garden walls. No. 48 Commando lost half its men here. The local cemetery houses the ashes of two Allied soldiers. A memorial stone dedicated to the 48th Royal Marine Commando stands in a square along the sea wall.

Saint-Aubin-sur-Mer

During the night of August 3rd to 4th 1940, Maurice Duclos, known as Saint-Jacques, returned to his town, sent by General de Gaulle to estimate the German forces present and their installations. As at Luc-sur-Mer, this beach had been visited by a British commando making a reconnaissance raid during the night of September 27th to 28th 1941. Less than three years later, the Canadian soldiers landed there. The North Shore Regiment encountered many problems, losing men and tanks on the beach because of German defences with a 50 mm cannon plus a large number of machine guns. After clearing the beach, the 22 amphibious tanks of the Fort Garry Horse came up against a pillbox. The 48th Royal Marine Commando landed during the second wave with the task of taking Langrune-sur-Mer. The soldiers killed on the Saint-Aubin beach are buried in the garden of a house near the sea wall. As for the school, it was used as a hospital. On the sea wall, just next to Bernières-sur-Mer, the Cassine battery remains. This stronghold was built on the grounds of a villa called La Cassine which the Germans knocked down to install several pillboxes linked by underground or open passages.

Near the battery a cannon can still be seen next to the monument dedicated to the No. 48 Commando, together with a list of civilian and military victims.

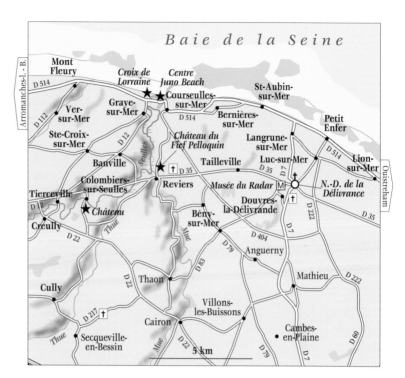

Bernières-sur-Mer, June 6th.

Bernières-sur-Mer

The Canadians of the Queen's Own Rifles and the Chaudière Regiment landed on this 1.5-mile-long beach. The beach looked like a forest of stakes because there were so many obstacles of all sorts. At 4 a.m., Bernières beach was heavily bombed. However, this town is situated in a sector where they live well, as an old Norman saying goes: *"If you want to be happy, go and live between Caen and Bayeux."* When the landing craft arrived at Bernières around 8.10 a.m., the Canadians had only about 100 yards between them and the beach. They landed under a hail of artillery shells. Ninety ships were destroyed, many beaching on the Bernières islands. The inhabitants of this town were surprised when they were liberated on June 6th at 9.30 a.m. to hear the "Tommies" speaking French or singing "I have come back to see my Normandy," since many of them were youngsters from Quebec of Norman origin who joined up to liberate the Old Continent. Several confirmed their French origin by shouting: *"I'm not English but French Canadian."* At 11.45. a.m. Major

Commemorative monument, Bernières-sur-Mer.

General Keller set up his command post in the Hôtel de la Plage. And it is from there that the first reports for agencies and international newspapers were written.

As soon as it was liberated, Bernières beach quickly piled up with tanks, trucks, tankettes and cannons.

Douvres-la-Délivrande

Near this town, famous for its Notre-Dame basilica and its annual festival in honour of the Black Virgin, on the road to Basly, was a German radar station with code-name *Distelfink* (Goldfinch). About a mile from the sea, this post could survey any naval operations coming from Britain. The ensemble comprised two Freya-type radars, one of the Wassermann type with a range of 190 miles and two of the Würzburg type. The post was protected by anti-aircraft defences and anti-tank cannons and had a telephone exchange, a radio station, an electric generator and an ammunition bay. But on June 6th, the Allies managed their jamming so well that even the last Würzburg radar that had withstood all the air bombardments did not see the naval armada arriving. However, the station stood up to Allied attacks for eleven days. The garrison of 238 men surrendered on June 17th after gas was injected into the ventilation holes of the bunkers: the information had been provided by French conscripts who had taken part in building them.

Today, the site serves as the first Radar Museum. It demonstrates the role of radars and their technological development. A clear scenography explains the work of air or sea equipment. Outside one can see a "Würzburg Riese" radar. After having been recuperated by the British in 1944, three radars were given to

Canadian cemetery in
Bény-Reviers.

the French Navy, then to a physics laboratory. In 1957, two were transformed into radio-telescopes for the Nançay station. The museum site shows one of these pieces of equipment out of the 1,500 built by the Germans after August 1941.

Douvres-la-Délivrande, liberated on June 6th, served as the headquarters of the Canadian Major General George Francoeur. The Vierge-Fidèle monastery was turned into a hospital. At the entrance to Douvres, coming from Caen, there is a British cemetery with 1,123 graves of combatants killed on the Sword and Juno beaches.

Bény-Reviers

On the road from Bernières to Bény, the Fief Pelloquin, a castle inhabited by the Hettier de Boislambert family, one of whose members had joined General de Gaulle in 1940, became the first Anglo-Canadian field hospital. Even though Bény-sur-Mer was well defended by the Moulineaux battery comprising four 100 mm guns

 Radar Museum

Route de Basly, 14440 Douvres-la-Délivrande, +33 (0)231377443
www.douvres-la-delivrande.fr
In 1942, a Würzburg radar was installed in the town of Douvres-la-Délivrande, which overlooks the English Channel. This radar was used for the remote detection of movements at sea. Today, the radar station – the only one of its kind on the Lower Normandy coast – is open to visitors, who can learn about the history and role of radars through documents and models on display in two bunkers.

Würzburg radar, Douvres-la-Délivrande.

Canadian soldiers and tanks in
Courseulles-sur-Mer.

and located in the town of Fontaine-Henri, it was liberated by the Chaudière Regiment on June 6th and an airstrip was built there. The Moulineaux battery was bombarded before 6 o'clock in the morning by the cruisers *Belfast* and *Diadem*. Between the towns of Bény-sur-Mer and Reviers there is a Canadian cemetery of 15 acres with 2,049 graves.

The neighbouring communes of Anguerny and Tailleville were also liberated on June 6th by Canadian soldiers. The telephone exchange set up in the castle was taken by the Canadian 8th Brigade. The castle later became a leave centre for Canadian soldiers.

Courseulles-sur-Mer

This little fishing port known for its oysters saw several Canadian units land on June 6th, in particular the First Hussars, the Regina Rifles, the Royal Winnipeg Rifles and the 1st Canadian Scottish.

The landing there was especially difficult. The regiment of Centaur tanks lost 34 out of the 40 that had landed. Held down under heavy fire from two pillboxes, one company lost two thirds of its men. The fierce fighting of the Regina Rifles, which had to advance house by house and street by street, liberated the town at about 10 a.m. At 8.30 a.m. the tank of sergeant Léo Gariépy of the First Hussars had attacked the *Kommandantur*. On the right bank of the estuary of the Seulles a Sherman DD (Duplex Drive) tank stands on a base; this

Juno Beach Centre, Courseulles-sur-Mer.

 Juno Beach Centre
Voie des Français Libres, 14470 Courseulles-sur-Mer,
+33 (0)231373217
www.junobeach.org
The Juno Beach Centre, which opened in 2003, is the only Canadian museum in Lower Normandy. It is located on the sea front among remains of the Atlantic Wall, near the beaches where the Canadian 3rd Infantry Division landed on June 6th 1944. It tells the story of Canada's involvement during the Second World War, emphasising the civilian and military war effort of an entire population. The Juno Beach Centre also contains exhibits about Canada as it is today.

vehicle weighing 32 tons was sunk on June 6th and has been placed there in memory of the landing of the Canadian 2nd Armoured Brigade and dedicated to Léo Gariépy. Further on, on the banks of the Seulles, there is a German gun complete with cannon and set in a concrete emplacement.

From June 8th, the mouth of the river Seulles gave shelter to the first Allied supply port before the artificial port of Arromanches had been completed: 2,000 tons of supplies were disembarked each day. Twelve ships were sunk in order to form an artificial roadstead. To the east of the jetty there is now a huge sword made out of teak; a monument dedicated to the Royal Winnipeg Rifles. The Juno Beach Centre pays tribute to the commitment of Canadian troops during the Second World War.

Sherman DD, Courseulles-sur-Mer.

Cross of Lorraine.

Arrival of General de Gaulle on French soil.

Graye-sur-Mer

The Royal Winnipeg Rifles, whose soldiers were nicknamed the "black devils", quickly took Graye-sur-Mer around 9 o'clock. But the sanatorium, defended by several Russian artillerymen, held out until the following day. Between Courseulles and Graye, General de Gaulle arrived on June 14th 1944 aboard the destroyer *La Combattante* to set foot on French soil again, accompanied among others by Generals Béthouart and Kœnig, and Maurice Schumann. The flag with the Cross of Lorraine from *La Combattante* is kept in Courseulles. A monument in the form of the Cross of Lorraine recalls this moment.

General de Gaulle left the Graye breach by Jeep to go to Creullet castle to meet Montgomery, who had landed here several days earlier. Several pillboxes still remain on this beach, which was also chosen by Winston Churchill and King George VI, who landed here on June 12th and June 16th respectively.

At the exit from the beach, at the foot of the Cross of Lorraine, stands an AVRE-Churchill tank called "One Charlie" from the 79th Armoured Division, which was recovered in November 1976.

On June 6th at about 5 p.m. an operating theatre was set up in the kitchen of the Sainte-Thérèse holiday camp, to care for the wounded whose numbers were growing by the hour. On July 4th, the hospital was transferred to the sanatorium: at the beginning of the battle of Falaise this hospital received 2,700 wounded in a single day.

Creully

The Canadian soldiers advanced quickly inland, liberating the villages of Tierceville, Colombiers-sur-Seulles, Sainte-Croix-sur-Mer, Banville, Villons-les-Buissons and Le Fresne-Camilly on their way, before reaching Creully. General Montgomery set up his first headquarters at Sainte-Croix-sur-Mer before transferring it, the same day, to Creullet castle, which was lower down. Creully was liberated on June 7th at about 5.30 p.m. and served as a link-up point for the Canadian and British armies coming from the Gold and Juno sectors.

Creully castle, built between the 12th and 16th centuries, had already been occupied by the English in 1417. In 1944, the BBC installed a studio there for direct transmissions to London. On the door of the 12th-century tower hung a notice "BBC, silence please. No entry". The transmitter on the top of the tower broadcast every day in the months of June and July. Thus the journalist Chester Wilmot could cover the Battle of Normandy for the BBC. The castle contains an exhibition of equipment and photographs taken by English, Canadian and French journalists.

From the terrace, there is a view of Creullet castle. In the castle grounds, between June 7th and 22nd, Montgomery installed his mobile headquarters camouflaged by stacks of hay. In the great salon of the castle, he received General de Gaulle, King George VI and Winston Churchill.

The Canadian soldiers had completed their task of settling in on the Calvados coast by taking a supply port, Courseulles-sur-Mer. Twenty-four thousand men were disembarked with 2,000 vehicles. Losses were less than a thousand. Apart from setting up this solid beachhead

they had advanced inland as far as Creully where they linked up with their British comrades who had landed on Gold Beach. But their advance to the east, towards Caen, was to be stopped for a month at the airfield of Carpiquet.

Château de Creully.

German prisoners.

51

Gold Beach

At 7.05 a.m., on the 3 miles of beaches between Ver-sur-Mer and Asnelles, 25,000 men landed from the 50th Northumbrian Infantry Division, accompanied by the 8th Armoured Division. The Northumbrian had proved itself during the French Campaign in May 1940, and then again in 1942 at El Alamein and in 1943 in Sicily. Among their motivations was revenge for the retreat from Dunkirk in 1940. General D. A. H. Graham was assigned the task of setting up on the cliffs overlooking Arromanches and quickly taking the town of Bayeux. General Graham told his soldiers: *"All of you, officers and men of the 50th Infantry Division, have the honour of having been chosen to strike this formidable blow for freedom."* In the Gold sector, the British used "funnies": tanks with chain whips in front which could blow up the mines on the beaches, while others could destroy the pillboxes or were equipped with an anti-sinking system. The tankdozer removed the obstacles placed on the beach whereas the "crocodile" was the most frightening with its flame-thrower. The landings were a great shock for the locals: as

an inhabitant of Arromanches, Mlle Lenglet, wrote in her diary: *"Nothing has changed in Arromanches, but from Saint-Côme and Courseulles one only sees ships, a wonderful and unforgettable sight which compensates for our previous hours".*

Ver-sur-Mer

The landing took place at 7.25 a.m. in the Rivière hamlet without any great problems, so much so that an hour later, the British troops had advanced half a mile inland and the site was cleaned in the following hours. The fusiliers of the 5th East Yorkshire then went on to the Mont Fleury battery half a mile away. The village of Ver-sur-Mer, decorated in 1948 by the Military Cross, pays homage to the 2nd Hertfordshire Battalion. The America Gold Beach Museum shows the victorious assault of the 69th brigade of the Northumbrian in the King sector. It is in memory of all the soldiers who landed at Ver-sur-Mer and liberated Bayeux. In the town is a house where Admiral Ramsay installed his headquarters. From above or from the coastal road leaving the village, one can see the high Arromanches cliffs.

British soldiers in the village of Ver-sur-Mer.

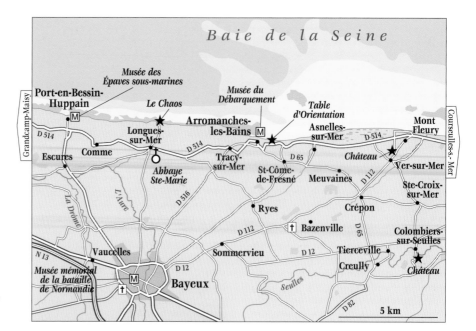

America Gold Beach Museum

Centre Saint-Exupéry, 2 place Amiral Byrd, 14114 Ver-sur-Mer,
+33 (0)231225858
www.goldbeachmusee.fr
This museum, situated in the centre of the town, tells the story of two major events that took place in the 20th century: the first mail-carrying flight between the United States and France on July 1st 1927, and the landing of the British 50th Division on June 6th 1944 in the Gold Beach sector. The museum particularly focuses on the work of the British secret service in preparing for the landings, with a host of documents, maps and photos on display.

To the west of Ver-sur-Mer, under Mont Fleury castle, the Mont Fleury battery was installed, with four Russian 122 mm guns, two in pillboxes and two in the open. The range of this battery was 9 miles. To the south-east was the Mare Fontaine battery equipped with four Czech 105 mm cannons installed in cube-shaped pillboxes. These two batteries, which could cover the whole of Gold Beach with their fire, were destroyed by bombing from the air and by fire from the cruisers *Orion* and *Belfast,* and mopping up operations were carried out in the morning of June 6th by soldiers of the 6th and 7th Green Howards. Sergeant Major Stan Hollis was given the only Victoria Cross awarded on D-Day. This soldier showed great bravery by capturing two blockhouses and saving the lives of two soldiers under enemy fire. Two pillboxes overgrown with greenery can still be seen at Mont Fleury.

Commemorative monument, Crépon.

Beach defence, Asnelles.

Asnelles-sur-Mer

The 1st Hampshire Regiment of the 231st Brigade landed on this beach, but throughout the whole of June 6th it met with fierce opposition from the German defences installed in small fortifications in Hamel. The rest of the 231st Brigade landed further east and met with less resistance, since the Russian soldiers were unmotivated and fled as soon as the firing started. Thanks to their "funnies", the British soldiers cleared the terrain, reached Meuvaines and occupied the strongholds overlooking Arromanches.

The coastal road crosses the village of Meuvaines, where the German artillery command post for shore defences was installed. An airstrip was set up there. Since 1998, at the far end of the new little cemetery, stands the isolated tomb of Maurice Schumann, spokesman for the Free French.

Commemorative plaque.

Maurice Schumann (1911-1998)

A journalist, he joined de Gaulle in 1940. In July 1940, he made a daily broadcast in French on the BBC, becoming the spokesman of the Free French. After landing at Asnelles, he arrived at Bayeux for the liberation of the town. Later, with the FFI (French Forces of the Interior) he took part in the liberation of the right bank of Caen. He was awarded the distinction "Companion of the Liberation", and entered politics after the war alongside General de Gaulle. He was elected member of parliament, then senator; he served as Minister for Foreign Affairs from 1969 to 1971. In 1974, he became a member of the Académie française. He is buried at the cemetery in Asnelles.

Top left: **Base of a Würzburg radar, Arromanches.**
Top right: **Würzburg radar in 1944, Arromanches.**

Notre-Dame-des-Flots.

Saint-Côme-de-Fresné

Before arriving in Arromanches-les-Bains, there is a panoramic table on the cliff with an excellent viewpoint over the Gold beaches to the east and the remains of the artificial harbour. This is the site of a former German radar station surrounded by concrete gun emplacements for anti-aircraft defences. This radar station was installed on the Arromanches cliffs together with a Freya-type long-range detection device, a Würzburg-type radar and two others which were more powerful: a Mammut and a Wassermann. Their range could go up to 50 miles, but these radars were destroyed by aerial bombardments several days before June 6th. After several hours of fighting, Saint-Côme-de-Fresné was liberated in the afternoon. The panoramic table gives a clear idea of the location of the artificial harbour of Arromanches by showing where the ships were anchored.

Close to the panoramic table there is a statue of Notre-Dame-des-Flots. It was knocked off its pedestal by the Germans so that it could no longer serve as a reference point, and was re-erected after the war looking towards Arromanches, doubtless to thank Notre-Dame-des-Flots for her protection during the landings.

There still remain German pillboxes on the Saint-Côme-de-Fresné cliff.

At the exit to the town stands the artillery command post for the coastline from Caen to Grandcamp-les-Bains.

Arromanches-les-Bains

In order to defend this small tourist fishing port, the Germans built a pillbox on the cliff overlooking Arromanches and another on the Tracy-sur-Mer cliff.

Liberated at 6 p.m. by land, by tanks arriving from Saint-Côme-de-Fresne, this small town, together with its neighbour Vierville, was chosen by the Allies for the creation of two artificial ports intended to provide supplies for the landing troops while awaiting the capture of a major French port. Since the failure of the Dieppe expedition, there

was no longer any question of taking over a harbour as such. The idea was to create one.

The two artificial ports, Mulberry A and B, were prefabricated in England and towed into place at 5 mph. They were and

remain a technological challenge. On June 7th, the Arromanches artificial port or Mulberry B, known as "Port Winston" after Winston Churchill whose idea it was, began to be put into place. To begin with, seventeen ships were

Unloading equipment in the
artificial port of Omaha Beach.

Aerial view of the artificial
port of Arromanches.

Place du 6 Juin, 14117 Arromanches les Bains, +33 (0)231223431
www.musee-arromanches.fr, www.arromanches-museum.com
This museum, set up by the D-Day Commemoration Committee, was inaugurated in 1954 by French President René Coty. It was built on the site of the artificial harbour, whose remains are still visible, and was the first museum to commemorate the landings of June 6th 1944. Working models and a film produced by the British admiralty explain how Port Winston was installed and operated. The museum also gives a general overview of the events surrounding the D-Day landings, particularly by means of a diorama.

Phoenix blocks at the west breakwater of the port of Arromanches.

sunk at sea to form a breakwater of blockships called Gooseberry. Next, 115 "Phoenix" blocks representing 500,000 tons of concrete (each block being 200 ft long, 60 ft high and 50 ft wide and weighing 6,044 tons) plus a dozen pontoons or jetty heads were arranged so as to compose a huge artificial roadstead comprising 10 miles of routes. Mulberry A located at Vierville was for the American troops whereas Mulberry B was intended for the British troops. But the storm of June 19th to 22nd destroyed the Vierville artificial harbour, so much so that the supply

D-Day Museum, Arromanches.

operations had to be regrouped in Arromanches. The assembly time took almost a fortnight. At the same time, routes were traced out and the beaches cleared. Once this was finished, the ensemble as a whole represented a roadstead over 5 miles long able to harbour the biggest ships. On June 12th, just six days after the landings, over 300,000 men, 54,000 vehicles and 104,000 tons of supplies had been disembarked. This harbour quickly became more efficient than Cherbourg or Le Havre: during the 100 days it was used it disembarked 2.5 million men, 500,000 vehicles and 4 million tons of equipment and supplies. The port was protected from a possible German air attack by 150 anti-aircraft guns and by permanent barrage balloons.

These days, there are still several pontoons to be seen from all points of the coast.

The D-Day Museum explains how artificial ports were built and operated. It also shows the different phases of the liberation of Normandy. Each Allied nation has a display window.

Top left: **Broken Phoenix block, east breakwater of the port of Arromanches.**
Top right: **Concrete floats washed up on the beach.**

Arromanches 360.

 Arromanches 360,
Chemin du Calvaire,
14117 Arromanches-les-Bains,
+33 (0)23123030
www.arromanches360.com
Arromanches 360 is located opposite the remains of the artificial harbour. It was built in 1994 and is the only circular cinema in France. It shows an eighteen-minute film entitled *The Price of Freedom*, which combines archive and present-day images on nine screens in a cinema that can seat 250 people. Visitors can learn about pontoons, the Pointe du Hoc, the bunkers and Omaha Beach.

Battery Museum

Tourist Information Centre, 14400 Longues-sur-Mer,
+33 (0)231214687 www.bayeux-bessin-tourism.com
The battery at Longues-sur-Mer, part of the Atlantic Wall, overlooks the English Channel from a 215 ft cliff: it covered the sectors of Gold Beach and Omaha Beach. It is the only coastal battery to be listed as a Historical Monument and is one of the rare examples that remains intact with its command post, its four pillboxes and ten protective Ringstands (or Tobruks), housing two 150 mm guns.

Firing direction post in the Longues-sur-Mer battery.

Longues-sur-Mer

This spot offers a superb range of vision over the sea from an altitude of 215 feet and was naturally chosen by the Germans in September 1943 to install a battery of four 150 mm guns with a range of up to 12.5 miles. In front of this battery, 300 yards away, on the edge of the cliff, was the observation post.

This battery was one of the dozen on the Normandy coast to open fire on the British fleet. The battery was heavily bombarded on May 28th and June 3rd, but without any destructive effect. Despite another intense pounding by 124 planes of the Royal Air Force, dropping 600 tons of bombs in the night of June 5th to 6th, the Longues battery resisted and opened fire at 5.37 a.m. on two American warships including the battleship *Arkansas*. Its firing range covered the two Allied sectors of Gold and Omaha, which made this battery especially dangerous for the landings. The decisive attack came from the sea, since the positions of the battery were known from information from the Resistance. The warships *Georges-Leygues, Montcalm, Ajax* and *Arkansas* took turns to fire on the battery and managed to destroy three of the four guns. The battery was put out of action completely just before 7.00 p.m. by two shots from the *Georges-Leygues* battleship and occupied the following morning after the garrison surrendered.

The road leading to the cliff, concreted by the Germans, gives a view of the whole of the battery: three of the four pillboxes have been preserved with their artillery. Each pillbox measures 15 yards by ten. The roof slab and the walls are 6 feet thick, which protected the guns aimed at the sea.

The pillboxes were half hidden by a thick layer of earth. The ensemble was protected by machine guns, mines and layers of barbed wire. This is the only Atlantic Wall battery kept in this state with its guns in their firing chamber. Above the guns, one can see big conduits which are the remains of a ventilation system intended to extract poisonous gases produced by the firing.

The ensemble, which remains the best example of a naval artillery battery, now belongs to the French Coastal Conservation Commission and is protected by the Historical Monuments list.

After Longues-sur-Mer, the coast road leads to Le Chaos. One can also take the cliff path starting from the Vauban tower at Port-en-Bessin. Here one can see a well-preserved system of German defences as well as a firing direction post located ahead of the battery 300 yards from the edge of the cliff, complete with a telemeter to control the firing range.

Cliff in Longues-sur-Mer. Natural site known as "Le Chaos".

Commemorative monument,
Port-en-Bessin.

Port-en-Bessin

Overlooking the fishing port, beyond the Vauban tower, on the top of the 215 ft cliff there was an ensemble of German defences.

The town was liberated on June 8th by the 47th Royal Marine Commando after more than a day's resistance by the Germans and then, after June 14th, became a supply port: 1,000 tons of equipment and supplies were unloaded every day.

On June 25th it became the first land-based point for PLUTO – Pipe Line Under the Ocean – supplied by cargo ships anchored out at sea. By the end of August, 175,000 tons of fuel had been delivered, with daily highs of 8,000 tons. This pipeline, named "Minor System", was linked up to that from Sainte-Honorine-des-Pertes and connected at Saint-Lô to the "Major System" coming from the port of Cherbourg.

There is a plaque dedicated to the 47th Royal Marine Commando on the blockhouse beneath the Vauban tower.

At the entrance to Port-en-Bessin, in the village of Commes, there is a museum of underwater wrecks. Twenty-five years of research on the sea bed enabled Jacques Lemonchois to raise hundreds of wrecks and a range of equipment and personal objects from inside the ships sunk during the landings, from bells from the destroyers *Isis* and *Swift* to tubes of toothpaste.

Port-en-Bessin marked the end of the British sector and the beginning of the American sector, especially that of Omaha which was so deadly.

Museum of underwater
wrecks, Port-en-Bessin.

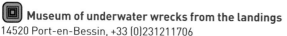

Museum of underwater wrecks from the landings
14520 Port-en-Bessin, +33 (0)231211706

This museum was founded in 1990 on the initiative of a diver, Jacques Lemonchois, who had been tasked by the government with cleaning the seabed and removing any wrecks that might hinder sea traffic. The museum displays remains from the D-Day landings found at the bottom of the sea. The exhibits, which have been specially treated so that they can be preserved, include a torpedo and a tank.

Bayeux

This town, 10 miles inland, is the only one in Normandy to have been completely undamaged, since it was liberated by British troops at 10 a.m. on June 7th. On June 12th, General Eisenhower visited the town with his son, who was on leave. At the end of the dual carriageway coming from Caen there is a roundabout paying homage to Overlord's Supreme Commander. A huge statue seems to welcome visitors.

Two days later, on June 14th, General de Gaulle arrived. Over two thousand people, happy to be liberated after four years of occupation, cheered him. He had come to set up the government of Free France with the appointment of the first government representative François Coulet and the first sub-prefect, Raymond Triboulet. In so doing, the leader of Free France affirmed his intention to assemble a French government and to thwart American aims to install their own administration: *"I want to make it clear immediately that every place abandoned by the Germans comes under the authority of my government".* On the square dedicated to the leader of Free France there is a column with this inscription: *"On this spot on XIV June MCMXLIV / To the inhabitants of Bayeux / Joyful in their deliverance / Charles de Gaulle / Liberator of the Homeland / addressed his first words / on the soil of liberated France".* This column recalls the intense joy felt by the inhabitants of Bayeux upon being liberated.

Two years later, General de Gaulle returned to Bayeux and gave his famous speech in which he laid out

De Gaulle in Bayeux, June 14th 1944.

63

Memorial Museum of the Battle of Normandy

Bd Fabian Ware, 14400 Bayeux, +33 (0)231514690
www.mairie-bayeux.fr

This museum, situated in the first town in mainland France to be liberated, houses a vast exhibition area that tells the story of the main episodes of the Battle of Normandy, from June 6th to August 29th 1944. The chronological display helps visitors understand the chain of events that took place, in particular through a series of illustrative maps. The themed displays contain a range of exhibits, including military uniforms.

Memorial Museum of the Battle of Normandy.

the foundations of the Constitution of the Fifth Republic. In June 1946, he declared: *"In our glorious but mutilated Normandy, Bayeux and its surroundings were witnesses to one the greatest clashes of history".* These days there is a memorial museum dedicated to General de Gaulle. It recounts the visits of the General to Bayeux through documents, photos, and film and sound tracks.

The biggest British cemetery in Normandy is to be found at Bayeux with 4,648 graves. On the other side of the boulevard a monumental portico has been built, with the names of 1,807 missing soldiers.

The Memorial Museum of the Battle of Normandy stands at the official limit of the British and American sectors.

On the evening of D-Day, the soldiers of the Northumbrian attained their objective, to occupy the shore between Corseulles and Arromanches

British cemetery in Bayeux.

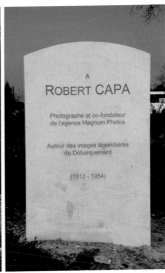

A

ROBERT CAPA

Photographe et co-fondateur
de l'agence Magnum Photos

Auteur des images légendaires
du Débarquement

(1913 - 1954)

and reach the outskirts of Bayeux, which was liberated the following day. At Creully they linked up with the Canadian soldiers who had landed on Juno Beach, but had to wait before they could join up with the American soldiers in difficulty on Omaha Beach. While they were waiting for the artificial port of Arromanches to be built, the Allies held two small ports to receive supplies; Port-en-Bessin and Courseulles. On June 8th, the Americans and British linked up: thus two days after the landings, the Allies controlled about 38 miles of coastline.

Top left: **Portico of the British cemetery in Bayeux.**
Top right: **Memorial stone in memory of photographer Robert Capa, Bayeux.**

Dwight David Eisenhower (1890-1969)

His nickname was Ike. He was second to MacArthur at the beginning of the war, and then named Commander-in-Chief of the Allied armies in North Africa in November 1942. He went from success to success, in Tunisia, Sicily and Italy. After the Teheran conference, he was promoted to Supreme Commander of the Allied Forces in Europe, in December 1943. His qualities as an organiser and diplomat were appreciated. On June 5th, he sent this message to the Allied soldiers: *"The eyes of the world are upon you, the hopes and prayers of liberty loving people everywhere march with you."* The landings were yet another success. On August 7th, he set up his mobile headquarters at Maisons, then on August 9th at Jullouville. After the liberation of Paris, he led the battle of the Ardennes, the German campaign and the freeing of the camps. He then entered political life and became Republican President of the United States from 1952 to 1960. He received an honorary doctorate from the University of Caen on November 13th 1948, the day the first stone was laid.

Eisenhower roundabout, Bayeux.

Omaha Beach

The first units of General Huebner, commander of the 1st Infantry Division nicknamed "the Big Red One", landed on the beaches leading to Sainte-Honorine-des-Pertes (Fox sector) up to the Percée headland (Charlie sector). This division was made up of experienced soldiers who had fought in North Africa and Sicily. The sector was also that of the 29th Infantry Division, Engineer Special Brigades and Ranger Battalions. Omar Bradley, commander of the 1st US Army, supervised the landings from the cruiser *Augusta*. The mission of the American soldiers was to take up positions on 6,500 yards of beaches defined at each extremity by 100 ft high cliffs and to establish themselves inland along a line formed by Isigny-Trévières-Vaucelles, following the RN 13 road. The beaches of Colleville-sur-Mer, Saint-Laurent-sur-Mer and Vierville-sur-Mer were the only ones suitable for a landing, as the Germans knew well, and consequently were well defended with small fortifications containing anti-tank weapons, 75

GIs landing at the foot of the Pointe du Hoc.

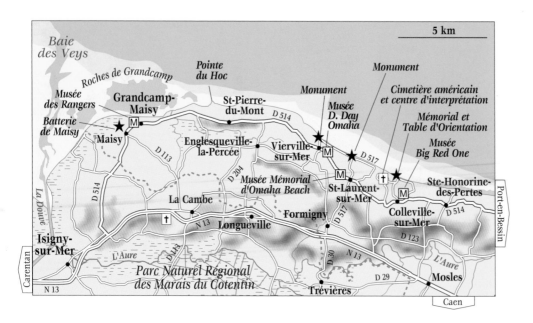

American soldier who survived the sinking of his ship.

and 88 mm cannons and machine guns placed behind a variety of obstacles, land mines and barbed wire networks. They were dominated by chalk cliffs and valleys. On June 6th, the sea was particularly rough, which made it difficult for the landing craft and for launching the amphibious tanks. At 4.30 a.m., 180 barges (Landing Craft Infantry) were released at about five miles from the shore, but high seas sank

several of them. The first ten ships sank but most of the soldiers were saved. As for their comrades, soaked, frozen and ill, they had to wait two hours longer before landing. While 29 Sherman DD (Duplex Drive nicknamed Donald Duck) amphibious tanks sank, the American troops tried to land under a deluge of German fire, caught under crossfire from machine guns and mortars. They had to cross about 600 yards of beach to find shelter under the sea wall. As soon as the soldiers set foot on the beach, they came under heavy fire. The GIs fell, company after company.

Omaha Beach, 6.35 a.m.

Charcoal drawing by Manuel Bromberg, who took part in D-Day as an official US army artist.

The war journal of the 116th regiment records: *"The enemy had awaited this moment. At the same time all our craft came under crossfire from its automatic weapons. Those men who instinctively jumped into the water to avoid the fire drowned immediately. There was total disorder... However, several managed to stay at their stations. Many were wounded and drowned. Very few reached the shore."* The German soldiers waited patiently in 85 little blockhouses which the GIs called pillboxes. The American general staff was unaware that the 352nd German Infantry Division, comprising elements from the eastern front, had chosen this sector for its manoeuvres, which doubled the German offensive. One hour after setting foot on the beach, the situation seemed alarming. The American soldiers could not advance. A report from the 5th Army Corps recorded a catastrophe at 7.30 a.m.: *"Our assault units are collapsing under our eyes. We have very heavy losses. Enemy fire prevents us from taking the shore."* Bedford village in Virginia lost 23 men on June 6th out of a total of just 3,000 inhabitants. Among them were the Hoback brothers, one killed and the other missing. Bedford is now twinned with Omaha Beach and plans to build a memorial.

Omaha Beach, a long beach of brown sand and pebbles bordered by a bank where yellow grasses grow, became *Bloody Omaha* in only a few hours. At 9 a.m. the situation seemed so critical that General Omar Bradley considered abandoning the landing operations. Colonel George A. Taylor, commanding the 16th infantry regiment, noted: *"There are two sorts of men left on the beach! The dead and those about to die! Let's get out of here, fast."* Then Omar Bradley ordered the fleet to bombard the German defences again. This vital decision enabled the soldiers to finally move forward,

especially since the Germans were beginning to run out of ammunition. The sappers were particularly courageous and managed to clear a large part of the beach. After several hours of fighting, they managed to establish a fragile bridgehead about a mile deep but at the price of 3,000 killed and just as many wounded or disappeared in the waves.

Sainte-Honorine-des-Pertes

This town, situated at the eastern end of Omaha, was subject to a reconnaissance raid during the night of September 12th to 13th 1942 within the framework of Operation Aquatint, but the twelve agents from the Secret Operation

Unloading of equipment on Omaha Beach.

THIS MARKS
THE SITE
OF FIRST
AMERICAN
CEMETERY
IN FRANCE
WORLD WAR II
SINCE
MOVED TO
AMERICAN
CEMETERY N. I

Emplacement du 1er cimetière américain
Débarquement de Juin 1944

1st Infantry Division
29th Infantry Division
5th Engineer Special Brigade
6th Engineer Special Brigade

Top left: Blockhouse still armed with its gun, Omaha Beach.
Top right: Memorial stone indicating the site of the first US military cemetery.

Executive making up the commando were killed. Despite the difficulties of the Omaha landings, the town was liberated on June 7th. At the beginning of July, its little port was one of the destinations of PLUTO in order to provide fuel for the American armies.

Colleville-sur-Mer

This small town was severely shelled until it was liberated on June 7th at about 10 a.m. after house-to-house fighting. The 1st and 29th Infantry Divisions took a

foothold there at the price of thousands of dead, wounded or missing on the beach defended by the "Pluskat" fortifications. A monument dedicated to the 5th Engineer Special Brigade has been erected on the remains of a blockhouse. Above this there is an obelisk monument in honour of the 1st US Infantry Division.

These days, the tranquillity of the beach, owned by the French Coastal Conservation Commission, is in stark contrast to the horrors of D-Day.

Omaha Beach today.

But this town, along with Saint-Laurent-sur-Mer, became known internationally because of the American cemetery built there by the American Battle Monuments Commission. It was inaugurated in 1956 by the President of the Republic, René Coty, and General Marshall. The 172-acre site, which has been given to the American Government in perpetuity, is located on the cliff overlooking Omaha Beach; this was the battleground of the right wing of the 1st Infantry Division. The cemetery houses the graves of 9,387 American soldiers killed in Normandy, including 307 unknown soldiers. The thousands of graves in white Carrare marble aligned perfectly on a trimmed lawn give the impression of greatness and beauty. The remembrance stones are in the shape of a Latin cross or the star of David. A father and son lie together and there are thirty-three cases of brothers buried together.

A circular chapel has been built out of Vaurion (Côte-d'Or) stone with steps in Ploumanac'h granite (Côtes d'Armor). The frieze is decorated with a replica of the Congress

 Military Cemetery Visitor Centre
14710 Colleville-sur-Mer, +33 (0)231516200
www.abmc.gov
The American cemetery in Colleville-sur-Mer was inaugurated in 1956. This 172-acre site overlooking Omaha Beach was granted in perpetuity by France to the United States. 9,387 soldiers are buried there. Since June 6th 2007, a Visitor Centre has been open to the public to pay tribute to the courage of the soldiers who were involved in the landings and to encourage visitors to reflect on the events of Operation Overlord.

Military Cemetery Visitor Centre, Colleville-sur-Mer.

American cemetery in Colleville.

Grave of Theodore Roosevelt, a distant cousin of President Franklin D. Roosevelt.

Monumental statue paying tribute to the courage of America's youth.

Big Red One Museum

Hameau Le Bray, 14710 Colleville-sur-Mer +33 (0)231215381
This small museum, located between Colleville-sur-Mer and Saint-Laurent-sur-Mer, was set up by a collector. It pays tribute to the 1st Infantry Division, known as the "Big Red One". It houses archives from June 1944, and particularly features an interesting film by a war correspondent.

medal and the altar is in Pyrenean marble. Above the altar, the grateful French have placed a laurel wreath for the soldiers who died for the Freedom of Europe. The roof mosaic, made by Léon Kroll from New York, symbolises America blessing its sons going to war. A time capsule containing newspaper articles from June 6th 1944 is enclosed there and will only be opened on June 6th 2044.

The memorial represents a semicircular series of columns in Vaurion stone; in the centre there is a monumental bronze statue 23 feet high created by Donald de Lue. It symbolises the spirit of American youth emerging from the waves and carries the inscription: *"My eyes have seen the glory of the coming of the Lord."* To the left of this monument is a belvedere overlooking the beach: a panoramic table shows the general map of the landings and explains the fighting for Omaha Beach.

There is a wall dedicated to the Missing in the garden in the form of an arc with 1,557 names. Not far away there is a pool with two flag-poles. A granite staircase offers a view of the cliffs, Omaha Beach and the Pointe du Hoc.

Homage is paid to the German soldiers of the 716th Infantry Division killed in Omaha by a cross at point WN 62.

Saint-Laurent-sur-Mer

Just like the other beaches of Calvados, that of Saint-Laurent-sur-Mer was subject to a reconnaissance raid by fifteen men during the night of January 17th to 18th 1942. Paradoxically, this beach was called Easy Beach for landing operations

Big Red One Museum, Colleville-sur-Mer.

while in fact it was a very difficult spot to win. A lieutenant shouted to his men: *"Are you going to stay there to be killed or are you going to get up and try not to be killed?"*

The village was liberated at 1 p.m. on June 6th. Not far from "Les Moulins" hamlet, where there is a commemorative stone, there still remains a blockhouse which served as the first headquarters in charge of organising the first exchanges between the beach and inland. In front of this there is a monument commemorating the landing of the 2nd "Indian Head" Infantry Division on June 7th. A memorial dedicated to the same division has been built on the Ruquet site. The first American airstrip was built near Saint-Laurent in order to evacuate the wounded.

On the seafront, just like on most of the landing beaches, there is a memorial monument dedicated to this event and built by the D-Day Commemoration Committee.

The June 6th 1944 Omaha Museum shows a collection of uniforms, vehicles, weapons and emblems. One can see a 155 mm cannon given by the United States Defence Ministry.

The Dog Red and Dog White sectors were established between Saint-Laurent-sur-Mer and Vierville-sur-Mer: it was here that General Norman Cota managed to link up men from different companies scattered by the tough fighting and to launch another assault on the German defences.

Vierville-sur-Mer

This sector of Omaha, called Dog Green, was the most deadly and the most confused. Not only did the landing craft sink with all their men aboard, but the tanks were hit by fire from the cannons from the Percée headland. Only a third of the

Signal Monument, Saint-Laurent-sur-Mer.

 Omaha Beach Memorial Museum
Avenue de la Libération, 14710 Saint-Laurent-sur-Mer,
+33 (0)231219744
www.musee-memorial-omaha.com
This museum, in the heart of the American sector of Omaha Beach, tells the story of the commitment of the American soldiers in this sector. Its exhibits include a large number of personal belongings, uniforms, vehicles and weapons. Photos and maps, together with soldiers' accounts, explain the complexity of the landing on Omaha Beach and the capture of the Pointe du Hoc.

Omaha Beach Memorial Museum, Saint-Laurent-sur-Mer.

National Guard monument,
Vierville-sur-Mer.

Elements of the floating jetty,
Vierville-sur-Mer.

180 soldiers of the A Company were able to continue; all their officers had been killed. The village was liberated at 11 a.m. on June 6th. At the far end of the road along the beach there remains a German pillbox, one of the defensive points which

prevented the American soldiers from leaving the beach. These days the blockhouse has a monument on top dedicated to the American National Guard in memory of its participation in two World Wars.

Elements of the jetty of the Mulberry A artificial port are still visible at low tide. This port, built on June 8th, was destroyed during the storm which hit the coasts between June 19th and 22nd. Eight hundred ships ran aground on the beaches. The sea's caprices delayed all the landing operations; Bradley's troops were running out of ammunition and the offensive planned for the 22nd on the Odon had to be postponed. Despite the damage, what remained of the artificial port made it possible to land 600,000 men and 104,000 vehicles before February 28th 1945. Some of the debris was used to repair the Arromanches artificial port.

A small monument below the road recalls that Vierville-sur-Mer was the site of the first American cemetery. It carries this inscription: *"This marks the site of the first American cemetery in France of World War II, since moved to American cemetery No. 1"*. The many dead on Omaha Beach were first of all buried in the sand and then, from June 19th, transferred to the Colleville-sur-Mer cemetery.

The village was taken on June 6th and the castle served as headquarters for the American army from June 8th to July 21st.

Englesqueville-la-Percée

The coast road leads the visitor to this village which housed a large radar station named Igel, in charge of watching the seas. The station was built on the Percée headland, a

 D-Day Omaha Museum
Route de Grandcamp-Maisy, 14710 Vierville-sur-Mer,
+33 (0)231217180
This museum, which houses a private collection, is devoted to the American landing on Omaha Beach. Its large exhibition area contains interesting exhibits explaining the technological progress made in wartime, together with elements of the artificial harbour destroyed by the storm in the middle of June 1944. Five floating causeways were presented to the public in 2004.

rocky spur similar to the Pointe du Hoc. It comprised a Freya-type radar specialised in marine surveillance plus two enormous Würzburg-type radars. After May 1944, these radars were silenced by the bombardments. The whole ensemble was captured by the 2nd Rangers Battalion on June 7th. Taking the fortified stronghold defended by two 77 mm cannons was especially difficult; only 29 of the 70 rangers managed to reach the top of the cliff. They needed support from naval artillery to silence the cannons at about 1.00 p.m. on June 6th. When the rangers reached the fortifications in the evening, they found the bodies of 69 German soldiers.

Pointe du Hoc

After passing Saint-Pierre-du-Mont where the German battery was bombarded in the afternoon of June 5th and neutralised on the 7th, the visitor reaches this splendid site of about 30 acres with its rocky prow

Storm on the mulberry.

Elements of floating roads warped by the storm.

Bombers of the 9th Air Force fly over the Pointe du Hoc on June 4th 1944.

pointing out to sea. The cliff, 100 feet high, had been thoroughly fortified by the Germans who had installed a battery there equipped with six French-origin 155 mm cannons on huge circular platforms open to the sky. This arrangement meant that the cannons could fire in any direction. Their fire, directed by an observation post at the edge of the cliff, had a range of 12 miles and could reach the east coast of the

Rangers climbing a cliff.

Cotentin peninsula. The German garrison was guarded by 125 infantrymen and 80 gunners protected by machine guns and well shielded in bunkers linked up by communication passages behind the barbed wire and the mines. The Todt organisation had begun building concrete pillboxes to house the cannons but the work was not finished in June 1944.

This stronghold was taken by storm by the 2nd Rangers Battalion commanded by Colonel James Rudder. The attack had been prepared by bombing during the night of June 5th to 6th: 700 tons of bombs were dropped by 124 planes in only a few minutes, while from the sea came a deluge of bombs and shells. The battleship *Texas*, in particular, fired over 600 salvoes of 356! The rangers had been specially trained for assault on the cliffs of the Isle of

the Pointe du Hoc, which the Allies called "Ho Point" on their maps. But the rangers had their ropes cut by the German defenders and came under fire from machine guns and hand grenades; 135 of the 225 were put out of action during the attack. The situation remained uncertain for 48 hours and it was only on June 8th at about midday that the battery was taken by the rangers.

The rangers had studied the site on aerial photos, but when they arrived they could not recognise anything since the terrain had been changed so much by the shelling and piles of concrete rubble.

The final victory came with the support of the 116th Infantry Regiment to which the ranger battalion belonged, backed up by tanks. The site, which has been preserved as it was, remains marked by the ferocity of the fighting, but this

Tip of the Pointe du Hoc.

Aerial view of the Pointe du Hoc.

Wight, using grappling irons, ropes, extensible rope ladders and even telescopic ladders lent by London's firemen. On June 6th at 7.10 a.m. 225 rangers in three separate companies landed at the bottom of the cliff of

victory was useless since the cannons had been dismantled several days before and replaced by big timber beams! The six cannons were hidden several miles away in an orchard behind apple trees.

The path leading to the edge of the cliff is now called "Colonel Rudder Alley". German and American bodies still lie under the rubble.

The land has been given to the American Government and has become a military sanctuary. At the very tip of the headland a monument has been built in the shape of a simple granite needle on the very site of the former firing direction post. On a cross planted in the earth one reads the following inscription: *"Here the combatants remain. In its chaos, the battle united them for eternity."*

Grandcamp-Maisy

At very low tide the sea uncovers a vast plateau of chalk rocks called the Roches de Grandcamp, extending for 5 miles from the Pointe du Hoc to the beginning of Veys Bay. The village of Grandcamp-les-Bains, turned into a

Gun platform, Pointe du Hoc.

Colonel J. Rudder.

James Rudder (1910-1970)

James Rudder, nicknamed "Big Jim", was a farmer, played American football and then became a trainer in Texas. From June 1943 he commanded the 2nd Rangers Battalion. He was victorious at the Pointe du Hoc and was awarded the DSC medal for his courage. He was later promoted to Brigadier General and received the Légion d'honneur. After the war he was elected President of Texas A&M University. He returned to the scene of his exploits in 1964 as a member of the US delegation led by General Bradley at the ceremonies held to mark the twentieth anniversary of the D-Day landings. He died on March 23rd 1970.

 Pointe du Hoc,
14450 Cricqueville-en-Bessin,
+33 (0)231519070
www.cc-isigny-grandcamp-intercom.fr
This site, perched on an 80 ft high vertical cliff between the sectors of Omaha Beach and Utah Beach, commemorates the victorious assault on June 6th to 8th 1944 by the 2nd Rangers Battalion, commanded by Colonel James Rudder, to take out the German battery. The land was given to the United States by France in January 1979. Visitors to the site can see blockhouses and a striking lunar landscape littered with bomb craters.

◻ Rangers Museum

Quai Crampon, 14450
Grandcamp-Maisy,
+33 (0)231923351
This museum, a few miles
from the Pointe du Hoc, pays
tribute to the Rangers under
Colonel Rudder who
captured this position on the
morning of June 6th. It
presents the history of this
Rangers Battalion created
on June 19th 1942 in
Northern Ireland, with
various objects and uniforms
displayed to illustrate the
soldiers' commitment.

Rangers Museum, Grandcamp.

◻ Maisy Battery

Route des Perruques, 14450 Grandcamp-Maisy,
+33 (0)678045625, www.maisybattery.com
This German battery on Route des Perruques was rediscovered at
the beginning of the 21st century. It covered the sectors of Omaha
and Utah. It was captured on June 9th following attacks by American
Rangers and five hours of intense fighting. The emplacements of six
gun platforms can be seen, together with tunnels and one mile of
trenches.
Platform of the Grandcamp-Maisy battery.

defensive stronghold by the
Germans, was liberated on June 9th.
General Bradley set up the headquarters of the 1st US Army there and
General Eisenhower stayed there
from July 1st to 5th.

The village of Maisy, located further away from the coast, was
defended by the batteries of La
Martinière and La Perruque. These
two batteries controlled the estuary
of the river Vire, one with three 100
mm guns and the other with six 155
mm guns with a range of 12 miles.
They were a direct threat to the sector of Utah on the east coast of the
Cotentin peninsula, and were put out
of action in the afternoon of June 6th
by the cruiser *Hawkins* and occupied
on June 9th.

A Rangers Museum has been set up
to pay tribute to the action of these
troops. At the entrance to the town
stands a monument dedicated to the
National Guard.

La Cambe

This village was initially the site of
an American cemetery with 4,534
graves which later were transferred

to the United States or to the Colleville-sur-Mer cemetery. These days, extending over 5 acres, there is a German cemetery with 21,202 graves. One enters through a porch which also acts as a chapel. Each soldier's name is inscribed on a small stone set in the closely-mowed lawn. The stone crosses are in groups of five on the grass. In the middle of the cemetery there is a tumulus 20 feet high topped by a granite cross with two statues at its sides: it contains the bodies of 296 non-identified German soldiers.

Isigny-sur-Mer

This town was supposed to be taken on June 6th, but the German defenders resisted along the RN 13 road. On June 9th the taking of this important centre for the dairy industry at the bottom of Veys Bay by the 29th US Infantry Division allowed the Omaha and Utah sectors to be linked up. But this only happened at the price of heavy bombing and great destruction, with 60% of the town being destroyed. Omar Bradley declared: *"The people of Isigny had waited for more than four years to be liberated. And now, seeing the ruins of their country, they consider us as responsible".* On General-de-Gaulle Square, in the middle of the town, a monument set up by the D-Day Commemoration Committee recalls the speech the head of Free France pronounced to the population on June 14th.

By the evening of June 6th, the Americans had lost over 3,000 soldiers, but 30,000 were established in a narrow bridgehead one-and-a-quarter miles deep (originally planned to be six and a quarter miles deep!). The powerful and efficient naval artillery out at sea moved in to 800 yards from the shore and managed to unblock a situation which Bradley had thought

German military cemetery in La Cambe.

compromised at one point. The site of Omaha Beach will always remain the most tragic, as shown by the American cemetery of Colleville/Saint-Laurent. Omar Bradley holds up his soldiers as an example: *"Each man who set foot on Omaha Beach that day was a hero."* Luckily, the following days saw an improvement: on June 8th the American soldiers linked up with their British colleagues who had landed at Gold Beach.

Funeral monument.

General Omar Bradley (1893-1981)

Second-in-command to Eisenhower in North Africa in 1943 and greatly respected by his soldiers, he commanded the 11th Army Corps in Tunisia and Sicily, and then the 1st Army during the landings. He was a good tactician, and organised Operation Cobra. On August 1st, he was promoted to head the 12th US Army Group in Germany. He was later named Chairman of the Joint Chiefs of Staff. He retired in 1953. He published his memoirs, *A soldier's story*, in 1952.

Utah Beach

American soldiers sheltering at the foot of an anti-tank wall before resuming the offensive.

Top: Utah Beach is cleaned after the landing.
Bottom: A deceased GI.

This was the fifth and final landing sector of D-Day, and the second American sector, but the only one situated in the département of Manche. The mission of the 7th Army Corps, commanded by General J. L. Collins, was to take the coastal positions and establish a solid bridgehead. That of the 4th Infantry Division of General R. O. Barton, whose second-in-command was General Teddy Roosevelt, was to establish themselves on the roads on the embankments above the flooded land and to link up with the 82nd and 101st Airborne Divisions parachuted after midnight over Sainte-Mère-Eglise. The 101st had the task of clearing the terrain between the sea and Sainte-Mère-Eglise whilst

the 82nd was to take this town and the bridges over the Merderet and Douve rivers. In order to protect Utah Beach, the American paratroopers quickly took the Varreville dunes. Once these positions had been established, the American troops which had landed in the Utah and Omaha sectors linked up and in ten days advanced towards Cherbourg, about 30 miles away.

The Utah sector had a special role to play in Operation Overlord. If the landing operations failed on one of these beaches or even on all, the general staff had planned to send everyone to this sector. The mission was to cut the Cotentin peninsula in two. Therefore the Utah landing had to succeed. The landing took place

Landing at Utah Beach.

Memorial stone in honour of the US marines involved in D-Day.

at 6.30 a.m. but one-and-a-quarter miles further south than intended. It was the least bloody of all the five sectors, with only 200 dead, since the attack had been well prepared by aerial bombing followed by fire from the warships. The entire sector was defended by five batteries, one of them very powerful, at Saint-Marcouf, and by a number of small fortifications at Saint-Martin-de-Varreville, Audouville-la-Hubert, La Madeleine, Beau Guillot and Le Grand Vey. At about 2 a.m. a thousand ships carrying 30,000 men and 3,500 vehicles approached the beaches of the eastern coast of Cotentin.

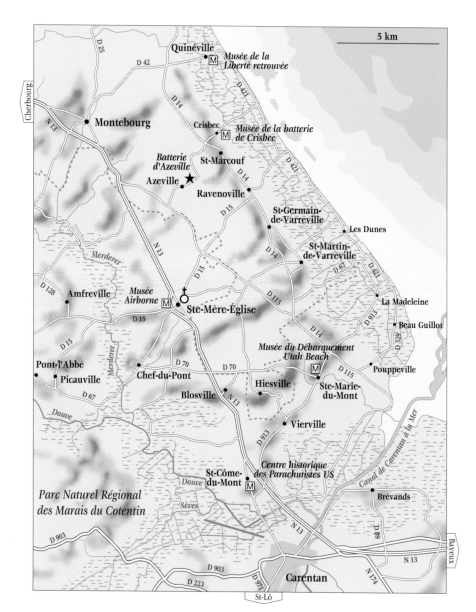

5 km

Quinéville
Musée de la
Liberté retrouvée
D 42
D 25
Cherbourg
N 13
Montebourg
Crisbec
Musée de la batterie
de Crisbec
D 14
D 421
Batterie
d'Azeville
St-Marcouf
D 14
Azeville
Ravenoville
D 421
D 15
St-Germain-
de-Varreville
Les Dunes
Merderet
D 14
St-Martin-
de-Varreville
D 128
Amfreville
N 13
Musée
Airborne
D 15
Ste-Mère-Église
D 67
D 421
D 913
La Madeleine
D 115
Beau Guillot
D 329
Merderet
D 15
D 14
Musée du Débarquement
Utah Beach
Pont-l'Abbé
Picauville
D 70
D 70
Chef-du-Pont
Hiesville
D 115
Pouppeville
D 67
Blosville
N 13
Ste-Marie-
du-Mont
Douve
Vierville
D 913
Canal de Carentan à la Mer
Centre historique
des Parachutistes US
St-Côme-
du-Mont
Parc Naturel Régional
des Marais du Cotentin
Douve
Sèves
Brévands
N 13
D 89
Bayeux
D 903
D 903
N 13
N 174
D 223
Carentan
D 971
St-Lô

Bottom left: Ringstand (or Tobruk) keeping watch on the beach.
Bottom right: Pillbox defending Utah Beach.

Sainte-Mère-Eglise

On June 6th, at about 1 a.m., 15,000 paratroopers from the 82nd and 101st Airborne Divisions, commanded respectively by Generals Matthew B. Ridgeway and Maxwell D. Taylor, were dropped above and around this town. The former had had experience of Sicily and Salerno, while the latter were inexperienced.

But the parachute drop was not precise enough, so much so that only 6,000 soldiers were in a position to fight. Many were scattered, for example General Maxwell Taylor. The furthest away landed near Barfleur, but others were drowned, tangled in their parachutes or sinking under the weight of the heavy equipment they were carrying. The survivors found each other using a little metallic toy imitating the song of the grasshopper. Unfortunately for some soldiers, the sound was similar to that of the German Mauser rifle! By sending its reserves to look for the scattered paratroopers, the German general staff made the landing on the beach

Steeple of Sainte-Mère-Eglise.

 Milestone 0 on "Liberty Highway"

Milestone 0 leads from the town hall of Saint-Mère-Eglise to "Liberty Highway", inaugurated on September 16th 1947. Milestone 00 is on Utah Beach and leads to La Madeleine to link up with Bastogne, 715 miles away.

These milestones symbolically mark the itinerary of the American army as it advanced towards the liberation of Europe and led to Bastogne in Belgium. These milestones can be divided between four sectors:
— sector 1 from Sainte-Mère-Eglise to Cherbourg (milestone 58). The Cherbourg stone is set at the junction of the France and Normandy quays;
— sector 2 from Sainte-Mère-Eglise to Avranches via Carentan, Saint-Lô and Villedieu-les-Poêles;
— sector 3 from Avranches to Metz;
— sector 4 from Metz to Bastogne.
Not far from Sainte-Mère-Eglise, the commune of Vierville was also liberated on June 6th.

Milestone on "Liberty Highway", Sainte-Mère-Eglise.

Stained glass window in the church of Sainte-Mère-Eglise.

Airborne Museum, Sainte-Mère-Eglise.

 Airborne Museum
14 Rue Eisenhower, 50480 Sainte-Mère Eglise,
+33 (0)233414135
www.musee-airborne.com
This museum is dedicated to the American 82nd and 101st Airborne Divisions, who were dropped at Sainte-Mère-Eglise and in the surrounding area during the night of June 5th to 6th 1944. A Waco glider and a Dakota C-47 "Argonia" are on display in two separate buildings. Uniformed figures and vehicles can also be seen. An original film entitled *Battle for Liberty* is shown to visitors. A 19,000 sq. foot extension is currently being built.

Emblems of the 82nd and 101st Airborne Divisions.

Commemorative plaque.

easier. The paratroopers of the 82nd Airborne were more precise than their comrades of the 101st; three quarters of them landed within a square of 3 miles. They managed to take Sainte-Mère-Eglise, defended by the 91st Division of the Luftwaffe, at 4.30 a.m., two hours before the landing. This conquest made it possible to cut the RN 13 road between Carentan and Cherbourg. The American flag which was flown that night at Sainte-Mère-Eglise was the same which had previously been flown over Naples. The paratroopers then unhooked their comrade John Steele who was still caught by his parachute on the steeple of the church and was wounded by German fire. These days there is a dummy figure attached to the church to recall this event.

Inside the church there are stained glass windows showing the arrival of the paratroopers at Sainte-Mère-Eglise. The window above the portal representing the paratroopers around the Virgin Mary is the work of master glass-maker Loire based on drawings by Paul Renaud.

This town housed the first American cemeteries: cemetery No. 1 with 2,195 graves and cemetery No. 2 with 4,811 graves. In the latter, Brigadier General Roosevelt was buried on July 14th. Later, these dead were transferred to Colleville-sur-Mer or repatriated to the United States.

In memory of the actions of the American 82nd and 101st Airborne Divisions, a paratrooper museum has been built near the church. The first stone of the building, whose roof is in the shape of a parachute, was laid by General Gavin in 1962.

Model from the Utah Beach Landing Museum.

 Utah Beach Landing Museum
La Madeleine, 50480 Sainte-Marie-du-Mont, +33 (0)233715335
www.utah-beach.com
This museum was created in 1962 by the mayor of Sainte-Marie-du-Mont. It is located on La Madeleine beach, at the heart of the Utah Beach sector. The museum was built in an old blockhouse, and has since been regularly renovated. Documents, military staff maps, equipment including amphibious vehicles and weapons and historical accounts take visitors back in time to the events of June 6th 1944. The museum offers a panoramic view of the beach.

German defence hidden in the dunes, Utah Beach.

Sainte-Marie-du-Mont

This old town, dominated by its Norman church, was occupied very early on by the paratroopers of the 101st Airborne led by General Maxwell Taylor. The La Madeleine beach has become famous by the name of Utah Beach. A stained glass window in the church recalls the episodes of the liberation of the village on June 6th.

On June 6th at 6.30 a.m. the 4th US Infantry Division landed by mistake on the "Grande Dune" hamlet, whereas the landing had been planned for more than a mile to the north, opposite the Varreville sand dunes. The 57-year-old cousin of the President of the United States, General Theodore Roosevelt, walking stick in hand, landed with the first wave and decided to continue operations. He justified his presence by telling General Barton: *"It will reassure the boys to know that I am with them."* The La Madeleine sector was one of the least defended, which made the landings easy not only for the men but also for the equipment. Therefore, the 33-ton Sherman DD tanks could go into action quickly while the engineers' bulldozers cleaned the beach. The Germans were severely hit by preventive bombardments: they tried to send Goliath miniature tanks filled with explosives, but only one exploded. A huge obelisk, erected thanks to contributions from veterans of the US 4th Infantry Division, commemorates the action of these soldiers near the remnants of the German pillboxes. Close by, a column in pink granite, 30 feet high, was erected *"by the United States of America in humble tribute to its sons who lost their lives in the liberation of these beaches. June 6, 1944".* This column was inaugurated on June 5th 1984 by General J. L. Collins. There is also a third monument dedicated to the soldiers of the 1st Engineer Special Brigade.

Following a suggestion by General Gaffey, 59 panels remembering the dead of this Engineer Brigade have been placed where they were killed.

Finally, a memorial stone recalls the landing of the 90th Infantry Division.

A Landing Museum has been set up in a blockhouse of the Atlantic Wall.

Each of the streets of this hamlet is named after soldiers or officers killed on June 6th; there is a stained glass window in the chapel made by the stained-glass artist Pierre Marie dedicated to Sainte Madeleine, which evokes the French forces inland: *"In the year 1944, the Free French forces took part in the landings with the Allied troops."*

On the road from La Madeleine to Sainte-Marie-du-Mont stands a monument, the work of the Danish sculptor Svend Lindhart, dedicated to the 800 Danish sailors who took part in the landings. The fortifications of Beau Guillot can still be seen around half a mile from La Madeleine.

Bottom left: **Monument to the 90th Infantry Division.**
Bottom right: **Panel dedicated to the 1st Engineer Special Brigade.**

A crashed glider in Hiesville.

General Maxwell Taylor, Commander of the 101st Airborne Division.

Pouppeville

This tiny hamlet, next to Sainte-Marie-du-Mont, was home to a German command post which supplied the strongholds of the sector. It was therefore vital to take it, as Gilles Perrault emphasises. The capture was delayed, however, because the paratroopers in charge had been scattered. Local resistance had prepared for their assault by cutting the telephone cables. The men of the 101st left Hiesville at 6 a.m. and controlled the hamlet by midday. The Pouppeville bridge was the point where the airborne troops and those who had landed on La Madeleine beach that morning linked up.

Hiesville

This village, about 4 miles from Sainte-Mère-Eglise, was liberated on June 6th by the paratroopers of the 101st, backed up by 32 Waco gliders. The latter brought in the reinforcements and equipment needed to consolidate their positions. Some gliders crashed on the stakes erected by Rommel. A hospital was set up in the Colombières manor. A temporary cemetery was built there before being transferred to the neighbouring commune of Blosville.

Blosville

This village, liberated on June 7th, housed a temporary cemetery with the graves of 5,622 American soldiers, victims of the terrible and deadly war of the hedges. These bodies were later transferred to the Colleville-sur-Mer cemetery.

Picauville-Chef-du-Pont

Chef-du-Pont was one of the priorities of the 82nd Airborne with the taking of the Merderet bridge and was conquered after three days of fighting, on June 9th. The Luftwaffe 91st Division had installed its tactical command post in Picauville castle. But its commander, General Falley, who had left for Rennes but returned, was killed in his car on June 6th by three American paratroopers.

Amfréville

The 82nd Airborne chose the zone surrounding this village for their landing, but the flooding of the marshes made it difficult. The paratroopers were scattered and had enormous difficulty in meeting each other with their "grasshoppers". The village was only liberated on June 12th after fierce fighting.

Carentan

This town is the only point in the Manche département where it was possible to cross the marshes towards Bessin, by the Grand Vey ford. It was only liberated by the 101st Airborne on June 12th. The town was bombarded on the morning of June 6th and again in the afternoon. On June 10th the American soldiers tried in vain to cross the four bridges. The taking of the town was marked by terrible fighting on the Carentan highway and the square of Choux when the 502nd Airborne Division advanced along the old RN 13 road.

Dead Man's Corner Museum, Saint-Côme-du-Mont.

 The D-Day Paratrooper Historical Center
2 Village de l'Amont, 50500 Saint-Côme du Mont,
+33 (0)233420042, www.paratrooper-museum.org
Since 2005, the Dead Man's Corner Museum has been open to the public in a house on the site known by US troops as "Dead Man's Corner". This historical centre pays tribute to the commitment of American paratroopers in the violent battles leading up to the liberation of Carentan on June 12th 1944. The realistic recreations of soldiers in action creates a unique atmosphere.

The Americans enter Carentan.

Crisbecq Battery Museum

Route des Manoirs, 50310 Saint-Marcouf-de-l'Isle,
+33 (0)668410904
www.batterie-marcouf.com
This 10-acre site, part of the Atlantic Wall constructed from 1941 onwards, contains 21 blockhouses. From this point, the Germans kept watch over the English Channel from Saint-Vaast-la-Hougue to the Pointe du Hoc, particularly the Utah Beach sector. The 210 mm guns housed here sunk the American destroyer *USS Corry*. In 2004, the site was turned into a museum about the history of the battery.

The Vareville dunes

This site should have been that of Utah Beach, but the landing craft drifted about one-and-a-quarter miles because of the strong currents owing to the bad weather, and arrived on La Madeleine beach.

Near this offshore bar, the villagers of Saint-Martin-de-Varreville saw the landing of General Leclerc and his 2nd Armoured Division of 15,000 men and 4,000 vehicles. A monument in pink granite in the shape of a ship's prow with the emblem of the Cross of Lorraine recalls this landing. Near the monument there are two vehicles carrying the emblem of the 2nd Armoured Division.

The coastal road known as the "Road of the Allies" runs along the Utah Beach sector. The dunes were defended by several batteries. That of Saint-Martin-de-Varreville, comprising four 105 mm cannons, was bombarded in the night of June 5th to 6th, but the guns had been dismantled. The battery was quickly taken by the American soldiers.

Tank from Marshal Leclerc's 2nd Armoured Division, Utah Beach.

Ringstand (or Tobruk) keeping watch on Utah Beach.

The naval battery of Crisbecq (named after the hamlet) at Saint-Marcouf, the biggest in the Seine bay after that of Le Havre, comprised four 210 mm cannons with a range of 17 miles, but only three were in working order. Their firepower was able to sink an American destroyer on June 7th. The battery covered a sector from Veys Bay to Saint-Vaast-la-Hougue. The ensemble as a whole was defended by a garrison of 400 men equipped with cannons and machine guns. All around there were anti-tank obstacles, mines and barbed wire. As Rémy Desquesnes noted, Crisbecq was the centre of gravity of German defences on the Cotentin eastern coast but, as a result, it was bombed the most.

This battery, overlooking the beaches of Ravenoville and Saint-Germain-de-Varreville, resisted all the bombardments and various assaults of the American paratroopers and the American 4th Division until June 12th when the Germans decided to withdraw. A huge shelter for a 210 mm cannon can still be seen. However, most of the pillboxes were destroyed by specialists from the Engineer Corps: they exploded them to test possible weaknesses in these constructions.

Pillbox beach defence, Utah Beach.

Pillbox on Ravenoville beach.

 Azeville Battery

La Rue d'Azeville, 50310 Azeville, +33 (0)233406305
www.patrimoine.manche.fr

This battery was built from 1941 onwards and was captured on June 9th 1944 by US soldiers. The site is run by the Manche General Council and has been open to the public since 1994. 1,150 feet of underground passages linking the pillboxes demonstrate the blockhouse architecture and the system of camouflage used for the battery. Visitors can watch a film about the construction of the Atlantic Wall and the relationship between the occupying forces and the occupied population, as seen through the accounts of those living in the village of Azeville.

Pillboxes in the Azeville battery.

At the hamlet known as "Les Campagnettes", two-and-a-half miles from the sea, was the Azeville battery, comprising four 105 mm cannons with a range of 6 miles. It acted as back-up for the Crisbecq battery. It was taken by flame-throwers on June 9th by soldiers of the 22nd Infantry Regiment. These days one can see two cells with a cistern on top to house a cannon.

Quinéville

This town marked the northern limit of the Utah sector, but also the furthest point of the American Cotentin advance by the evening of June 15th. The King of England James II left from here to take part in the Battle of La Hougue in 1692. During the night of December 25th to 26th 1943, this sandy beach had been visited by a British reconnaissance commando. It was defended by the Morsalines battery equipped with six 155 mm cannons. Bombed by Allied planes, it was evacuated by the Germans and its guns moved one-and-a-quarter miles away. This new position meant that the cannons could not reach La Madeleine beach, which was now too far away. The beach was cleared on June 15th after taking the Saint-Marcouf fort. By the evening of June 6th, the Americans had landed 23,500 men, 1,700 vehicles and 1,800 tons of supplies. Despite several centres of resistance such as Quinéville and the Saint-Marcouf and Azeville positions, a solid bridgehead had been established and the link-up with the 82nd and 101st Airborne Divisions had been made. The German defences in the Utah sector put up little resistance, so that at about midday on June 6th General Bradley received a reassuring message: *"Beaches cleaned, routes under construction, little opposition"*. It remained for all these American armies to start advancing towards the north of the département with the aim of cutting off the Cotentin

peninsula and above all of taking Cherbourg. The beaches of the Utah sector, sheltered from any German counter-attack, saw the landing of 836,000 men from forty divisions, 220,000 vehicles and 725,000 tons of supplies between the months of June and November 1944.

Memorial of Refound Freedom
18 Avenue de la Plage, 50310 Quinéville, +33 (0)233959595
www.memorial-quineville.com
This museum is unique in that it tells the story of the daily life of the people of Normandy from the Occupation to the Liberation, illustrated by wide-ranging displays of memorabilia. It features a reconstruction of a street with houses and shops, showing a queue in front of a butcher's. One room is devoted to women and children during the war. The museum contains a blockhouse from the Atlantic Wall. Visitors can also watch a film about the liberation of the Cotentin peninsula.

Pillbox in the Crisbecq battery, today.

Pillbox in the Crisbecq battery, June 1944.

The mission to take the port of Cherbourg

At the north of the Cotentin peninsula, Cherbourg was located in a wide gulf barred by a huge dyke separating a vast artificial roadstead. The American troops who landed on Utah Beach on June 6th had the mission of taking Cherbourg within ten days. But their advance was halted by fierce German resistance behind the woodland hedges and in front of each town or village on the way to Cherbourg. Each position had to be taken after fierce fighting. The American general staff brought in the 82nd Airborne Division, and the 4th, 9th, 79th and 90th Infantry Divisions. Their progress was extremely difficult, taking Chef-du-Pont on June 10th, Pont-l'Abbé on June 13th, Orglandes, Néhou, Saint-Sauveur-le-Vicomte on June 17th, and Saint-Jacques-de-Néhou and Barneville on June 18th. At this moment, the Cotentin peninsula was cut in two; General Collins led his offensive with his usual energy and installed thirty battalions.

Valognes

The little "Normandy Versailles" was bombed for three consecutive days; the 6th, 7th and 8th June. Many old town-houses were hit and 75% of the town destroyed. When Valognes was liberated on June 20th, the American soldiers of the

8th Infantry Division of Colonel Van Fleet entered a town in ruins and abandoned by its survivors.

Before this, they had launched an offensive on Orglandes in order to isolate the north of the Cotentin peninsula. The fighting lasted from June 15th to 17th, which demonstrates the ferocity of the German resistance. There is a German cemetery near this village, with 10,152 graves. The German soldiers who fell during the Cotentin fighting lie here. Their names are inscribed on the small stone crosses set in the green sward.

Valognes in ruins.

Montebourg

There is a local saying: "*Who holds
Montebourg holds Cherbourg*". Terrible
combats took place between
American and German troops in the
town, which was bombed on June
6th and most heavily on June 8th.
After these bombardments the
American soldiers attacked the town
on June 12th. Fierce German resistance meant that the assaults had to
be repeated over the following days.
The town changed hands several
times before being finally liberated at
3 a.m. on June 19th. On June 15th,
stopped in front of Montebourg,
General Joseph Lawton Collins stated that the *"main aim now of the army
corps must be to cut off the peninsula"*.
This aim was fulfilled on June 18th.
After that, progress was rapid: the 19
miles between Bricquebec and Les
Pieux took two days. The American
troops advanced towards the west via
Nehou and towards the south via
Saint-Sauveur-le-Vicomte, 75% of
which had been destroyed.

The taking of La Haye-du-Puits on
July 9th had been particularly deadly and was called "Bloody Hill". The
attack against Mont Castre on July
8th resulted in the death of 2,000
soldiers. Once the Montebourg
blockage had been breached, the
doors to the Val de Saire opened. On
June 20th in the evening, the troops
of General Manton Eddy arrived at
Cherbourg, ready to take the port if
necessary for the operations.

The Val de Saire comprised various defensive installations such as
the La Pernelle batteries. These batteries, established on a peak 410 feet
high, and equipped with 170 mm
cannons with a range of 19 miles,
covered the whole naval horizon
from the La Hague cape to Utah
Beach. On June 6th, Allied planes
dropped 668 tons of bombs. The
Germans did not want the cannons
to fall into the hands of the
Americans and destroyed them
themselves on June 19th. The
equipment of the radar station at

Saint-Pierre-Eglise remained intact. It was protected by the most powerful battery on the Cotentin peninsula, the Hamburg battery, which was equipped with four 240 mm guns. On June 25th an Anglo-American naval force attacked, but an air attack on June 28th was needed before the Germans surrendered. The Germans had planned to set up a V1 site at Hardinvast, to send 1/2 ton bombs over the south of England, but they did not have the time to build the metallic ramp. About twenty ramps were built in North Cotentin, but they were quickly detected by the French resistance, bombed and put out of action.

Cherbourg

On June 19th, three American units, the 4th, 9th and 79th Infantry Divisions, commanded by General Joseph Lawton Collins, guided by resistants from Cherbourg, launched the attack on Cherbourg. At the same time, the Germans began the systematic destruction of Cherbourg's port installations. The Hommet jetty was blown up on June 19th, on the 20th the forward port blew up, while ships were scuttled in the channels and the whole port was mined. On June 21st, General von Schlieben refused an offer of surrender.

The real battle of Cherbourg began on June 22nd with a massive air and naval pounding and continued with the encircling of the

Admiral von Schlieben surrenders in Cherbourg.

Generals Bradley and Collins.

General Joseph Lawton Collins (1896-1987)

Joseph Lawton Collins was nicknamed "Lightning Joe" because of the rapidity of his action in the Pacific Ocean against the Japanese. He graduated from West Point in 1917, and arrived in Europe the same year. He was then part of the occupation troops in Germany. He was promoted to General in 1942, and commanded the 25th Division at Guadalcanal. In December 1943, he was sent to Britain. He commanded the 7th Army Corps at Utah Beach. He took Cherbourg, and this excellent tactician drew up Operation Cobra. He was a dedicated military chief; he took the 7th Army Corps as far as the Elbe, and then discovered the concentration camps. He became spokesman of the War Ministry, and then Chief of Staff of the United States Army from 1949 to 1953. In 1954 he was named Ambassador to South Vietnam, but he retired in 1956.

Cherbourg fortress. On the 23rd, the maritime terminal was dynamited by the German army while the Americans arrived in Tourlaville and encircled Equeurdreville. On the 24th, American pressure became so

heavy that the Germans abandoned their destruction of the port. The final attack began on June 25th with a naval bombardment of the German defences. The 4th and 79th US Divisions occupied the east of the town. On the evening of the 25th, General Collins gave an ultimatum to General von Schlieben. On the 26th, American soldiers entered every district of the town of Cherbourg. By the end of the day, the town had been liberated. Admiral Henneke and General von Schlieben, who had been ordered by Hitler and Rommel to resist until the very last bullet, gave themselves up from their underground bunker outside Octeville. Ten thousand soldiers were taken prisoner with them. The official surrender was signed at Servigny castle, in the town of Yvetot-Bocage, where General Collins had his command post. The arsenal, the Maupertuis airstrip and the forts on the main dyke fell in the following days. The whole of the north of the Cotentin peninsula was completely liberated by July 1st.

On June 27th, in the town hall, General Collins solemnly handed over to the mayor a French flag made out of parachute material. The huge losses of the 7th Corps are evidence of the violence of the fighting: 2,800 dead, 3,000 missing and 13,500 wounded.

When the 7th Army Corps took possession of Cherbourg, it discovered that the port had been completely devastated, obstructed by about a hundred wrecked ships and infested with mines. The quays had been destroyed, the arsenal ruined and the sluice gates sabotaged. The first ship able to enter the port was a British minesweeper. And with it, a flotilla of American, Canadian and English minesweepers, frogmen from the Royal Navy and divers systematically cleared the roadstead.

They found every type of mine existing at that time: depression, magnetic and acoustic. Next the wrecks had to be re-floated. The port installations were roughly put back into working order in the record time of fifteen days, which is illustrated by the motto of the US 333rd Engineer Regiment: *"We do what is difficult immediately; the impossible takes a little longer"*. However, it needed three months of tireless work, day and night, to open up the port of Cherbourg completely. On July 16th, the first four Liberty ships entered the port. Cherbourg could take its place as the port the Americans needed to disembark the equipment, material and supplies required to continue operations in the Cotentin peninsula, which Gilles Perrault called *"the central nourishing artery of the Allied armies"*. On September 7th, 23,000 soldiers from the United States landed. From October 15th onwards, over 20,000 tons of equipment and supplies were unloaded daily. On November 2nd, with 133 posts available on the quay, Cherbourg became the biggest

A locomotive is unloaded in the port of Cherbourg.

Unloading of supplies and equipment.

port in the world with 1 million tons, before reaching 2 million tons in February 1945.

These figures demonstrate Cherbourg's strategic importance at the heart of the Allied organisation. Evacuation was carried out rapidly by railways which had been quickly repaired: on August 30th, the Cherbourg-Paris line was reopened, including lorries if necessary. From August 25th the front was supplied following the "Red Ball Express Highway", a route leaving Saint-Lô to end up eventually in Brussels. According to the expression of Robert Lerouvillois, it was *"the longest one-way track ever put into service in the world"*. Its maximum length was 1,500 miles there and back and it carried 410,000 tons of supplies in three months. From Cherbourg to Saint-Lô, this track joined the Liberty Track. Cherbourg also sheltered hospital ships and embarked 148,000 wounded.

Querqueville, a town in the Cherbourg built-up area, was the terminal of the PLUTO pipeline from the Isle of Wight, 70 miles away.

This was the first underwater pipeline in history, and the idea came from Lord Louis Mountbatten. From August 12th, it supplied the armies with fuel. It was tried out in the Severn estuary, between Swansea and Ilfracombe, but unsuccessfully. A second was put into operation on August 21st. On November 30th, it carried 1 million litres of fuel per day. The pipeline followed the progress of the armies as far as Dourdan. Later it was named the "Major System" and linked up to Germany.

PLUTO pipeline.

Mont Roule

Mont Roule dominates the Cherbourg area at a height of 360 feet. Robert Lerouvillois quotes an old saying illustrating the strategic importance of this hill: "*He who holds Roule holds Cherbourg*". The fort, built in the 19th century, was equipped with a battery of four 105 mm guns. By pointing their guns along the flank of the cliff at a height of 265 feet, they had a range of seven and a half miles. Despite the bombing, the fort resisted. It needed the courage of Corporal Kelly, a ranger from the 314th Infantry Regiment, climbing up the rocks, to place explosive charges inside the blockhouse and thus force the Germans to surrender. Lieutenant Ogden, who was just as courageous and belonged to the same division, advanced alone towards the German positions and destroyed them with hand grenades. After two days of fierce and bloody fighting, the Americans took control of Mont Roule, at 9.48 p.m. on June 25th, and planted their flag there.

These days, the fort houses the Cherbourg Liberation Museum, the

 Liberation Museum

Fort du Roule, Montée des Résistants, 50100 Cherbourg-Octeville, +33 (0)233201412 www.ville-cherbourg.fr

This fort, perched nearly 400 feet above Cherbourg and its harbour, dates from the time of the Second Empire. It was occupied by the Germans until June 25th 1944, when its capture led to the liberation of Cherbourg. The museum was created in 1954 and entirely renovated in 1994. The exhibits tell the story of Cherbourg from its invasion to its liberation; the basement area is dedicated to the Occupation. Various themes are presented, including passive defence and wartime games. Visitors can enjoy a stunning view of Cherbourg and the picturesque harbour.

first museum depicting the Battle of Normandy.

Three weeks after the landings on Utah Beach, the aim of the American armies had been achieved, with the capture of Cherbourg. The liberation of the north of the Cotentin peninsula provided the Allies with a dependable base and installed them definitively on the continent so that they could continue their operations to liberate the south of the Manche département. But the American armies paid a high price for their progress since their landing on Utah Beach: 22,000 dead, wounded or missing.

Liberation Museum, Cherbourg.

Central
and southern Manche

American soldiers in the hell
of the hedges.

Capturing Cherbourg was of very great importance because of the strategic and logistic interests of the port. Once this mission was accomplished by General Lawton Collins on June 26th 1944, the US troops disembarked all the equipment, material and supplies they needed to continue their operations. For his part, General Omar Bradley devised Operation Cobra. The aim was to leave the marshlands and break through the German front in the direction of Avranches. The US divisions were held back by the war of the hedges from the end of June. They attacked in order to break through the German defences from July 25th, with heavy shelling which destroyed many towns and villages.

The war of the hedges
The bushy hedges, thick copses, small hunting grounds, banks, ditches and narrow paths which crisscrossed the wooded landscape of the centre and south of the Manche

département were completely new to the American troops, most of them young inexperienced recruits. On the other hand, the German soldiers knew these copses and pastures well since they had been there for four years. Each hedge, each copse and each path represented a natural trap which made bloody guerrilla warfare possible. The German defences were organised into three lines: automatic weapons for the first, mortars for the second and cannons for the third. Four American army corps were involved in this hedges hell: the 7th led by General Collins between Carentan and Périers, the 5th commanded by General Gerow to the east of Saint-Lô, the 8th of General Middleton between La Haye-du-Puits and Coutances and the 19th under General Corlett between the Vire and Taute rivers in the Saint-Lô direction. The modern weapons of the American soldiers were ineffective: the shells were not able to pierce these hedges made up of bushy trees and thick scrub. The tanks had great difficulty in moving and manoeuvring. Every time a tank tried to climb a bank it became an easy target for the enemy. Besides this, the continuing bad weather of summer 1944 turned the land into an impracticable quagmire. In fact,

German soldiers lying in ambush.

Major Thomas D. Howie (1908-1944)

As Operations Officer of the 29th US Infantry Division, he landed at Omaha. He took part in the battle of Saint-Lô and was killed on the evening of July 18th by a shell exploding. He was wrapped in the American flag and carried to the ruins of the Sainte-Croix church by his men. He became the symbol of the American victims and their sacrifices during the terrible battle for the liberation of Saint-Lô. The American poet Joseph Auslander dedicated a poem to him entitled Incident at St-Lô: *"They rode him in, propped straight and proud and tall/Through St. Lo's gates..."*

only the infantrymen managed to advance in what became the hell of the hedges. But their progress was very slow and systematic, advancing field after field, orchard after orchard, hedge after hedge: the 8th Army Corps battled for twelve days and only moved seven miles forward! The soldiers advanced without knowing where the enemy was, and exposed themselves to deadly enemy

A moment of relaxation for the GIs.

fire. The tanks were eventually made more effective thanks to the idea of an American sergeant who fixed a sort of steel cutting plough to the front of the tank. This improvement turned the tank into a bulldozer, nicknamed "Rhinoceros", which could knock down the hedges and copses and flatten the banks. In mid-July, the four American armies stopped their slow progress, since it was costing too many lives: for a gain of three miles, the 8th Army Corps lost 5,000 men; as for the 19th Army Corps, for a gain of six miles it lost 6,000 men. The only town which was taken was La Haye-du-Puits after seven days of fierce fighting. This hell of the hedges lasted for more than four weeks until Operation Cobra, launched on July 25th, and its carpet bombing managed to free the bogged-down American armies and break through the German front.

Marigny-La Chapelle-Enjuger

In the night of June 5th to 6th, to attract the attention of the Germans, the Royal Air Force parachuted dummies filled with sand over Rampan, Marigny and the Lessay heath. On June 13th, the commune of Marigny was bombed and destroyed. When Operation Cobra was launched on July 25th, it attacked the front line. Sixty thousand tons of fragmentation, napalm or phosphorus bombs were dropped by more than 1,600 flying fortresses and 1,500 fighter-bombers, flattening the villages of La Chapelle-Enjuger, Hébécrevon, Saint-Gilles and Mesnil-Eury over an area of only 4 square miles. The Panzer Lehr was crushed under the bombs, as its commander General Bayerlein stated: *"My front line looked like a lunar landscape and at least 70% of my men were out of action, dead, wounded or in a state of shock".* After being liberated on July 27th, a temporary American cemetery was built

to house 3,024 graves until the Colleville-sur-Mer cemetery was created. Not far away, 4,000 German soldiers were buried in mass graves until the creation of a permanent cemetery in the communes of Marigny and La Chapelle-Enjuger: it contains 11,169 graves.

Périers-Coutances

Operation Cobra destroyed towns and villages in its wake: Périers was 80% destroyed and Coutances 65%. Coutances had already been flattened twice by bombing, on June 6th and June 12th. The town burned for several days. On July 26th, the road leading from Saint-Lô to Coutances was cut by the Americans at Saint-Gilles. Périers and Lessay were liberated on July 27th and Coutances the following day.

Saint-Lô

On June 6th the town was bombed. It came under 5,000 tons of bombs and 90% of the town was destroyed: it became the "capital of ruins". In fact, Saint-Lô was a vital communications centre and the command post of the 84th German Army Korps. During the bombardment of the 6th, the prison was destroyed, causing the death of 42 resistants including the sub-prefect of Cherbourg, Lionel Audigier.

On the morning of June 7th, Saint-Lô was in ruins, but still controlled by the Germans, who turned it into a resistance outpost to counter the American advance. On July 12th the American soldiers were halted on the heights surrounding the town and on the road linking Saint-Lô to Lessay. On July 17th the Americans

American soldiers in the ruins of Saint-Lô.

captured Pont-Hébert and occupied the hills overlooking Saint-Lô. On July 18th, the 115th US Regiment entered the town despite heavy losses. The fighting continued among the ruins for a whole week. On July 25th, General Bradley launched Operation Cobra: the Panzer Lehr front to the south of the road from Périers to Saint-Lô was wiped out under carpet bombing.

Although they had intended to capture the town a week after landing, the Americans only entered it forty-three days later. But this hard-fought victory allowed General Patton to launch the attack on Avranches on July 26th.

Visitors arriving from Bayeux reach a roundabout dedicated to Major Howie. His bronze bust symbolises the sacrifices of thousands of GIs who fought to liberate the town.

Beaucoudray

Between Villebaudon and Beaucoudray, at the "Ferme du Bois", the Post Office resistance unit of Saint-Lô took refuge. Carelessness meant that they were detected by a group of SS soldiers stationed nearby. After a short period of fighting, 11 resistants were captured on June 14th and shot the next day in a field where a monument has been erected.

Left-hand page
Saint-Lô, which became the "capital of ruins".

A US jeep enters Saint-Lô.

George Patton (1885-1945)

George Patton was nicknamed "Old Blood and Guts" by his soldiers, because of both his courage and his brutality. He was trained at the armoured cavalry school of West Point, and fought Pancho Villa in 1916. He was appointed aide-de-camp to General Pershing during the First World War. He was an advocate of armoured warfare and showed great audacity during the landing in North Africa in 1942, going on to command the 7th Division in Sicily. But after slapping a soldier he fell into disgrace and his colleague Bradley was chosen to lead the fighting in Normandy. He was given the command of the phantom army during Operation Fortitude before being called to Normandy in July 1944. On August 1st, his 3rd Army entered the battle with the breakthrough to Avranches and then advanced on Paris and the Ardennes. In March 1945 he was in Trier and he then entered Austria and Czechoslovakia: he cried upon discovering the concentration camps. He was appointed governor of Bavaria and then relieved of his post because of his anti-Soviet attitude. He published his memoirs, *War as I knew it*, and died in a car accident on December 21st 1945.

General George Patton.

Avranches

Avranches, famous for its library and its rich collection of manuscripts from the abbey of Mont-Saint-Michel housed in the Scriptorial, was bombarded for three days, on June 7th, 8th and 10th. On July 30th, a hundred German vehicles trying to counter-attack were destroyed by Allied bombing. The same day, Bréhal, Gavray, La Haye-Pesnel and Sartilly were liberated. General Patton's 3rd Army took the Germans from behind and liberated

US tanks entering Avranches, July 31st 1944.

Avranches on July 30th and 31st after a quick breakthrough. Even though he only held a single bridge, Patton managed to pass seven divisions in three days. He could therefore enter Brittany and reached Rennes on August 4th.

A monument dedicated to General Patton has been built on the very spot where he stayed. This park is American territory: the soil and the trees were brought from America.

Saint-James

This village, liberated on the same day as Pontorson and Tessy-sur-Vire, is home to one of the two American cemeteries in Lower Normandy. In a green setting stretching over 30 acres, one-and-a-quarter miles to the south-east, lie 4,410 soldiers from the US 3rd Army. The little marble crosses are dominated by a chapel topped by a steeple. This memorial chapel houses a collection of flags, and stained glass windows, emblems and maps portray the events of 1944.

Huisnes-sur-Mer

Overlooking the bay a few miles from the Abbey of Mont-Saint-Michel, which was miraculously preserved from the destruction of the war, is a German ossuary. There are 68 cavities which have housed the remains of 11,956 soldiers since 1963. At the centre there is a stretch of open green sward where a cross has been erected.

Mortain

This little town was the centre of the last, but terrible, German counterattack, in an effort to stop the advance of the American armies. Operation Lütticch, which Hitler wanted against the advice of von Kluge, the successor of von Rundstedt, who would have preferred to withdraw towards the Seine, involved launching a counterattack on August 7th with eight of the nine armoured divisions stationed in

Normandy. The Germans managed to recapture Saint-Jean-du-Corail, but failed when they reached Barenton. The following day, between Gathemo and Saint-Barthélemy, the fighter bombers of the Royal Air Force attacked the German tanks. General Barton's 4th Division resisted before taking them in a pincer movement, recapturing Saint-Jean-du-Corail on August 11th. Mortain collapsed under repeated bombing, especially that of August 12th by the Luftwaffe, the day it was liberated after hand-to-hand fighting in the ruins of the town. In the same way as the other towns in the area, 84% of Mortain was destroyed.

The taking of Mortain marked the complete liberation of the Manche département. But a heavy price was paid, with the deaths of thousands of US and German civilians and soldiers. The "war of the hedges" ended with more than 12,000 dead. When Operation Cobra was launched, the elite German armoured division, the Panzer Lehr, lost more than 1,000 men in two days. The carpet bombing technique from more than 3,000 planes allowed the Allies to take the initiative. Operation Cobra started on July 25th and allowed the American armies to reach Avranches on the 30th. General Patton, commanding the 3rd Army, quickly took advantage of the breakthrough made by the 1st Army.

American cemetery in Saint-James.

Chapel in Saint-James cemetery.

The Battle for Caen

The aim of the landings was to capture the city of Caen on the evening of June 6th, but the British armies did not manage to reach the capital of Lower Normandy. General Montgomery's troops were stopped to the north-west and west of Caen by solid German resistance on the Périers ridge and on the main road leading from Caen to Bayeux: forty tanks from the 21st Panzerdivision had taken up positions there. The young fanatics of the 12th SS Panzerdivision "Hitlerjugend", led by Colonel Kurt Meyer, a convinced Nazi, arrived from their base near Evreux and managed to take up position to the north of the city. The Allied armies attacked again on June 25th by a movement intended to encircle Caen from the south. In order to do this, they had to cross the rivers Odon and Orne and the battle cost them over 7,000 lives. Operation Epsom was stopped on July 1st after having brought in the major part of the German armoured divisions but failing to capture Caen.

Caen after the battle.

Abbaye aux Hommes and town hall in Caen, today.

Caen

On June 6th in Caen, at 2 o'clock in the morning, the 1,020th alert since the beginning of the Occupation sounded. This alert seemed as if it would never end, writes the deputy mayor of Caen, Joseph Poirier. During the violent bombing of June 6th and 7th, the centre of the city was destroyed and burned. Kurt Meyer, SS commander of the "Hitlerjugend", noted on June 7th: *"Caen is a sea of flames where civilians are wandering around in the ruins and the streets are blocked by rubble; it is almost impossible to breathe... From a military point of view, the destruction of Caen is an unspeakable folly."* But these same SS who criticised the destruction of Caen had themselves committed an unspeakable crime, shooting 70 to 75 prisoners in the prison yards at 10.30 a.m. on the day of the landings. Their bodies were never found. On June 8th, more than

Refugees in the cloister of the Abbaye aux Hommes, Caen.

4,500 inhabitants of Caen took refuge in the Malherbe lycée and the Abbaye aux Hommes. The Bonsauver home and the refectory of the abbey were transformed into a hospital. This whole group of buildings, which had become a sanitary refuge, was miraculously spared.

Two weeks later, their numbers had doubled. The bombing continued with the same violence, in particular on June 13th and 14th. Back in the month of April, General Montgomery had warned that if the Germans reached Caen before him the city would be bombed: *"If the enemy reaches Caen before us and if its defences turn out to be too strong for us to capture the city on D-Day, Caen will be pounded by our bombers so that it cannot be of use to the enemy."*

Throughout the month of June, the assaults of the British army failed against this city, two thirds of which had been destroyed. On July 7th, the city was violently attacked again: 450 Lancaster and Halifax bombers commanded by General Harris dropped over 2,500 tons of bombs on the northern part of Caen in less than one hour. Was this really necessary? For Alexander McKee, *"The 2,500 tons dropped from the air had no noticeable effect. If the British chiefs of staff had thought they could intimidate the Germans by killing French people, they made a huge error".* It was a massacre for nothing, ordered by General Montgomery; Eisenhower had begun to talk about a British setback at Caen and Montgomery, after several failures attacking Caen, decided to carry out this bombing on July 7th. "Monty" undoubtedly regretted this episode, since there is no mention of it in his memoirs.

Bernard Montgomery (1887-1976)

He was wounded in the First World War. On November 2nd 1942 he was put in charge of the 8th British Army, defeating Rommel at El Alamein and the Axis armies in Tunisia in May 1943. He then took part in the campaigns in Italy and Sicily. In January 1944 he became second-in-command to Eisenhower and modified the Overlord project. His armies fought fiercely to take Caen, and at a certain time his authoritarianism was disputed by his subordinates. He was promoted to Field Marshal on August 31st 1944. He commanded the British armies and several American divisions until the end of the war. From 1951 to 1958, he commanded the Atlantic forces in Europe.

General B. L. Montgomery.

Caen, Rue Saint-Jean.

 Caen Memorial

Esplanade Général Eisenhower, 14000 Caen, +33 (0)231060645
www.memorial-caen.fr

The Caen Memorial was founded by Jean-Marie Girault and inaugurated on June 6th 1988 by French President François Mitterrand and the 11 ambassadors of the countries that fought for freedom in 1944. This museum presents the history of the 20th century, taking visitors on a journey through time with a reflection on the future and focusing on three main themes: the Second World War, the Cold War, and the defence of human rights. Three new exhibition areas were opened in 2010: *World War – Total War*, *The D-Day Landings and the Battle of Normandy*, and *Opinion Spots*, which presents international events as depicted by press artists. Each year, the Memorial also features a major temporary exhibition.

Caen Memorial.

By now, three quarters of the city of Caen had been destroyed. One hundred and fifteen thousand British and Canadian soldiers launched yet another attack, and after two days of fierce fighting, on Sunday July 9th at 6 p.m. the Canadian soldiers made a breakthrough to the right bank. But all the bridges over the river Orne had been destroyed by the Germans. The left bank, where the German soldiers of the 12th SS Panzerdivision and 272nd Infantry Division were established, was only liberated ten days later, but 35,000 residents of Caen were left victims of the operation. The taking of Caen marked the end of Operation Charnwood carried out by the British 21st Army Group.

The Memorial for Peace, built on the site of the command post of General Wilhelm Richter who led the 716th Infantry Division, reminds visitors of the history of the entire 20th century. This post, installed in a chalk quarry, was entirely underground and closed by armour-plated doors. It contained the administrative services of the 716th Division, a map room, a radio station, a telephone exchange and various other technical installations. On the façade of the building, which is built in Caen stone, the following phrase is engraved on either side of the entrance: *"Pain broke me, brotherhood raised me up, a river of freedom flowed from my wound"*. The Memorial leads visitors along a carefully planned historical route, divided into three different areas, and helps them understand the major political and strategic issues of the 20th century. This museographic journey is illustrated by three audiovisual sections presenting two films and an animated map of the Battle of Normandy. The Memorial's commitment to peace is demonstrated by a gallery of Nobel Peace Prize winners. The International Park for the Liberation of Europe, with its American and Canadian gardens, is dedicated to the Allied countries.

Carpiquet

In 1941, the Germans built a concrete runway 1,000 yards long to facilitate the movements of their planes. Two young Caen residents, Jean Hébert and Denys Boudard, stole a German plane from here and flew to England. Because of its military and strategic interest, this aerodrome was one of the objectives of the Allied armies on June 6th. It was a failure, just like Caen. On June 18th, the aerodrome became one of the objectives of Operation Epsom, which was only launched on June 25th since it was delayed by the destruction of the artificial port of Vierville-sur-Mer. The aerodrome of Carpiquet was especially well defended by blockhouses in reinforced concrete, turrets equipped with machine guns, pillboxes linked by underground passages, 75 mm anti-tank cannons and 50 mm anti-aircraft guns. The whole ensemble was surrounded by many mines and lines of barbed wire. The town was also defended by cannons and machine guns. The complexity and extent of these defences were known to the Canadian soldiers thanks to intelligence from the French Resistance. The mission was assigned to the 5,000 men of the 8th Canadian Brigade of the Royal Winnipeg Rifles and the Fort Garry Horse tanks. From July 4th to 7th, Canadian soldiers and young fanatics from the 12th SS Panzerdivision "Hitlerjugend" took part in furious combats, often hand-to-hand, to take the airfield. The attack was launched at dawn on July 4th and the battle continued under a hail of shells fired from both sides. The first assault cost the 8th Canadian Brigade 477 lives. Even though they came under a deluge of artillery and mortar fire, the Canadians managed to hold their position and push back German counter-attacks. On July 7th, however, the situation seemed to be impossible, since the numbers of dead and wounded were rising endlessly. This hell lasted until July 9th. Finally, some positions were taken by flame-throwers.

Ruins in the main road of Carpiquet.

Ardenne Abbey

The Canadian soldiers took the towns of Buron and Authie on June 7th, but had to push back two SS attacks before giving up. Ardenne Abbey, about half a mile from Carpiquet, stands in a strategic position overlooking Caen. This abbey,

Bottom left: **Ardenne Abbey partially destroyed in 1944.**
Bottom right: **Ardenne Abbey, today.**

founded in the 12th century by Prémontré monks, had been fortified by the Todt organisation with the installation of pillboxes, and served as base for the German counter-attack against the Canadian soldiers, from June 7th. The combats to take this site were especially bitter because of the assassination of 18 Canadian soldiers by the young SS fanatics of the 12th Hitlerjugend under Kurt Meyer. The latter directed the movements of his tanks by coming and going on motorbike. The abbey was liberated on July 9th during Operation Charnwood. The town of Authie was liberated the same day after bloody fighting between Canadian and SS soldiers. The crime that took place at Ardenne Abbey was unfortunately not the only one to be committed against prisoners: on June 8th, 48 Canadian soldiers of the Queen's Own Rifles from Toronto had been shot by the Germans.

There is a small chapel in memory of the Canadian soldiers. It comprises a wooden cross with a niche containing a statue of the Virgin Mary. A Canadian army steel helmet is suspended from the cross. The children of Authie bring flowers to this chapel every year.

Commemorative monument at spot height 112.

Tourville-sur-Odon

This commune remains one of the most important places of the battle of the Odon during Operation Epsom launched by Marshal Montgomery with 60,000 men, 600 tanks and 700 cannons. The river Odon flows in a deep and narrow wooded valley, which makes it very difficult to cross. The attacks launched in an attempt to cross the Odon caused heavy losses among the British ranks. The 15th Scottish Infantry Division liberated this village on June 27th.

Spot height 112

This excellent observation point overlooking Caen was of great strategic importance. This sector was marked out to the south by the valley of the Orne and to the north by the river Odon. The battle of the Odon took place at its foot. On June 25th events began by a barrage of fire from land and sea in order to prepare for the attack of the 15th Scottish Infantry Division. Its progress in the mud and under the rain was made even more difficult by the fierce resistance of the Hitlerjugend. On June 26th the Tourmauville bridge was taken, which allowed the 11th British Armoured Division to launch an attack on the hill. But they were pushed back by the 1st SS Panzer. The Germans regrouped three tank divisions along a line from Gavrus to Cheux and attacked in turn, but without success. The fighting continued for nearly a month. On July 10th, the British made another attempt to cross the Odon, but were halted by the German defences. The Duke of Cornwall's Light Infantry finally managed to cross on August 4th, but at the price of 2,000 men. The hill changed hands ten times.

A monument at the crossroads of the D8 and D36 pays homage to the Dorset and Hampshire Battalions which were decimated during an attack launched from the Fontaine-Etoupefour castle by the Waffen SS.

Bourguébus

This town was the framework of Operation Goodwood, launched on July 18th. The conquest of the ridge overlooking the town involved violent combats between British and German troops. The attack had been prepared by heavy bombing from 4,500 planes which pounded the sector for three hours. The British sent in three armoured divisions including the "Desert Rats", but were pushed back by three German Armoured Divisions: Tigers and Panthers against Sherman and Cromwell tanks, which still remains the greatest tank-fight of the Battle of Normandy. The 7th British Armoured Division arrived at Bourguébus on July 20th. The same day, Montgomery stopped Operation Goodwood, which had cost too many men – 6,000 – and too much equipment – 400 tanks – just to progress 7 miles. Like all the villages around, Bourguébus was hit and destroyed to a large extent.

Tilly-sur-Seulles

Norey-en-Bessin, a vital point, was captured at midday on June 7th by the Reginas and served as the base for Operation Epsom. To the south, there now stands the British cemetery of Norrey-Saint-Manvieu. The battle of Tilly took place a few miles away. For eleven days, from June 8th to 19th, the 30th British Army Corps and the Panzer Lehr were locked in fierce combat. The Panzer Lehr had arrived with 190 tanks, but only 66 remained at the end of the clash. The German line of defence had held out, but at a great price! As well as its tanks, the Panzer Lehr had lost 5,500 men. The town changed hands twenty times and finally, on June 19th, was taken by the 50th British

Museum of the Battle of Tilly-sur-Seulles

Chapelle Notre-Dame du Val, 14520 Tilly sur Seulles, +33 (0)607594602 www.tilly1944.fr, www.museetilly.free.fr

This museum, housed in the 12th-century Chapel of Notre-Dame du Val, focuses on the violent battles that took place between June 9th and 26th 1944 in Tilly-sur-Seulles and the surrounding towns and villages. The historical events are illustrated by documents, photos and accounts from British soldiers, together with memorabilia recovered from the battlefield.

Museum of the Battle of Tilly-sur-Seulles.

Infantry Division. At Tilly-sur-Seulles there is a cemetery with 1,222 graves as well as a museum which explains the battle. Not far away, the little hamlet of Jérusalem, in the town of Chouain, houses the graves of 46 British soldiers, including that of soldier Banks, only 16 years old.

The end of the battle of Caen and the entry of the British armies into the plain pushed the Germans back towards Falaise and the south of the Calvados département, where the Battle of Normandy ended. The Epsom and Goodwood operations played their part in these decisive advances.

The copses
and pastures of Calvados

Panzer IV and Tiger tank in Villers-Bocage.

On July 25th, parallel to Operation Cobra launched by the American troops in the south and centre of the Manche département, and as a back-up, General Montgomery launched Operation Bluecoat from Caumont-l'Eventé on July 30th in the direction of Montpinçon and Vire. Two British Army Corps, the 8th and the 30th, were assigned the respective missions of taking Bény-Bocage and Saint-Martin-des-Besaces, before advancing towards Vassy. The British breakthrough in the bocage took the German counter-attack by surprise at Mortain and the battle of Falaise-Chambois began.

Saint-Martin-des-Besaces

This town was located at the limit of the British and American sectors. It was encircled on July 30th and liberated on the 31st at 11 a.m. by the 11th British Armoured Division.

The remains of violent combats.

Bocage Breakthrough Museum,
Saint-Martin-des-Besaces.

Villers-Bocage

The 7th British Armoured Division and the Panzer Lehr confronted each other here on June 13th. When a leading English tank came into the village, it was blown up by fire from the Tiger tank of SS Captain Michael Wittmann. He then knocked out the major part of the British tank columns: the "Desert Rats" were thus forced to withdraw, abandoning 25 tanks. This ace of tank combat, also responsible for the hangings of Tulle, clocked up 138 victories by the beginning of August. On

Bocage Breakthrough Museum
14350 Saint-Martin des Besaces, +33 (0)231675278
www.laperceedubocage.com
This museum, set up by a private founder, attests to its creator's gratitude to the area's liberators. Eight exhibition areas and a diorama with sound and light effects present the harsh battles fought by British troops in the bocage (the copses and pastures) during Operation Bluecoat, and also focus on the work of local Resistance members.

August 8th he was killed near Cintheaux. The British 7th Armoured Division, more used to desert conditions and rapid movements, reacted badly to the woodlands of the local terrain. After the war, it was severely criticised by General Dempsey: *"The 7th Armoured Division, relying on its reputation, carried out this battle dishonourably."* At least this episode persuaded the German tanks to move away from the Cotentin fighting.

During the night of June 14th to 15th, Villers-Bocage was heavily bombed in order to prevent the regrouping of German tanks. On June 30th, a new and terrible bombing flattened this little town, which had been already liberated on August 4th by the Northumbrian.

Aunay-sur-Odon

This town is also a crossroads and was therefore completely destroyed by aerial bombing, first on June 12th at 7 a.m. and then later between June 12th and 15th. Among the ruins, where two hundred inhabitants were killed during Operation Epsom, the first tank battle took place between the 7th Armoured Division and the 10th SS Panzerdivision. The flattened town was liberated on August 5th by the 8th British Army Corps.

Not far away, in the little town of Saint-Charles-de-Percy, there is a cemetery housing the graves of 792 British soldiers.

Mont Pinçon

This hill, 1,180 ft high, is steep and sharp. The foot-soldiers assaulted it on August 6th at about midday from the western slope. They came under intense fire from the German defenders. Six tanks managed to reach the summit and were quickly backed up by foot-soldiers from the 4th Wiltshire Regiment. It was very difficult for them to climb under the sun and through the bushes. This battle attracted the attention of the 1st and 9th Panzerdivisions, which weakened German forces around Caen.

Vire

This sub-prefecture was a major crossroads for routes to the south and the west. As a result of its position, Vire was almost totally flattened by British bombing. On June 6th, the town centre and the junctions of the roads from Caen to Rennes and from Paris to Granville were destroyed. The incessant bombing destroyed the town and its inhabitants fled.

The American soldiers had to conquer the hills overlooking Vire one by one. Two days of fierce fighting began on August 5th between the US 29th Infantry Division and the 2nd SS Panzer. After street fighting the town was liberated on August 7th. At the same time, Mont Pinçon was taken, but with difficulty. The last Germans left on August 8th, and the Allies saw that the town had been completely burned down and left in ruins, not only by their own bombing but particularly by the violence from the Germans.

Operation Bluecoat liberated the Calvados bocage, but only at the price of very heavy destruction, with most of the towns being flattened. The woodlands and pastures, with their uplands and downlands, prevented concerted manoeuvres and the fighting continued until mid-August. Thury-Harcourt was only liberated on August 13th and Condé-sur-Noireau on August 17th.

Vire after the bombardments.

The Pocket

The whole plain between Caen and Falaise was a huge battlefield. On July 7th, the 1st Canadian Army, commanded by Lieutenant-General Henry Crerar, launched an attack to the south which resulted in bloody fighting along the old D158 road. This battle ended with the Canadian soldiers taking Falaise on August 16th and 17th. The British and American armies, supported by Polish and French divisions, engaged in the last big battle for Normandy by encircling about 110,000 German soldiers in the Chambois Pocket.

Cintheaux-Langannerie

These two towns, liberated on August 8th and 9th, house two cemeteries. Near Cintheaux, on August 8th, Captain Michael Wittman was killed, and his Tiger tank was not found again before 1982. Langannerie houses the only Polish cemetery of the battle of

Surrender of a German
detachment, August 19th 1944
in Saint-Lambert.

Top left: **Polish cemetery in Langannerie.**
Top right: **Canadian cemetery in Cintheaux.**

Memorial stone in tribute to Gérard Doré, a Canadian soldier who died on July 23rd 1944 at the age of 16.

August 1944 Museum

Chemin des Roches, 14700 Falaise, +33 (0)231903719
This museum is housed in an old cheese dairy at the foot of the mediaeval castle. It tells the story of the battle of the Falaise Pocket, presenting the violent fighting that took place in August 1944 by means of reconstructions using uniformed figures and military equipment. Outside the museum, visitors can see a German gun and Sexton armoured vehicle.

Normandy, with 696 graves from the 1st Polish Armoured Division commanded by General Maczek. They were equipped with Sherman tanks involved for the first time in the Battle of Normandy.

Cintheaux houses one of the two Canadian cemeteries in Normandy. Just outside the town lie 2,958 soldiers.

Falaise

At the outlet of the Caen plain, this sub-prefecture became one of Normandy's martyr towns, 85% of it being destroyed by a succession of bombings over a period of more than two months. On August 7th, the Canadians attacked along the Caen to Falaise road during Operation Totalize. They had advanced by 5 miles by the evening of August 8th. But after two days they had to give up, 7 miles away from Falaise, since the 35 tanks of the 12th SS Panzerdivision were so resistant. During the night of August 13th to 14th, Operation Tractable was launched: 700 bombers dropped 4,000 tons of bombs on a town which had already been hit hard during the weeks before. After fierce fighting to take the hills overlooking the town, the battle to take the town began on August 16th. Two days of bitter fighting between Canadian and SS soldiers

August 1944 Museum, Falaise.

were needed for complete liberation. On the morning of August 17th the Canadian soldiers of the 6th Brigade entered Falaise, and the following day the Mont-Royal Light Infantry, backed up by flame-throwing tanks, evacuated the last Germans from the town.

The August 1944 Museum tells the story of this battle and is remarkable for its vehicles on display, in particular an Opel NSU caterpillar, a Kubelwagen Volkswagen and an English Lloyd Carrier.

Mont Ormel

This ridge, 3 miles north of Chambois, is formed of two twin hills at spot height 262, and was renamed "Maczuga" (many weapons) by the soldiers of the 1st Polish Armoured Division under General Maczek, who took it on August 19th. They established themselves there with 80 tanks and 1,500 men. This achievement enabled the Allies to control both sides of the Chambois to Vimoutiers road and especially to dominate the whole valley of the river Dives. However, the Polish soldiers remained separated from their Canadian comrades by a little valley leading to Vimoutiers. The breach allowed several thousand German soldiers to escape.

A monument dominates the whole region and the valley of the Dives; this high wall in light-coloured stone recalls the events of 1944. A tank and an armoured car are set at spot height 262.

The MontOrmel Memorial, overlooking a site of exceptional beauty, recounts the complete history of the Pocket and commemorates the bloody battles there. There is a sound and light show lasting seventeen minutes.

Patrol of Canadian soldiers in the ruins of Falaise.

 Montormel Memorial
Les Havettes, 61160 Montormel, +33 (0)233673861
www.memorial-montormel.org
This museum is devoted to the last great battle in Normandy, the battle of Chambois. It is set in the heart of the battlefield overlooking the valley of the Dives, which can be seen through large windows. The museum was opened in 1994; it is built into the hillside which was occupied by Polish tanks on August 19th 1944. An animated relief map tells the story of this decisive battle, which ended in the "Corridor of Death".

Montormel Memorial.

Bust of Abbot Launay, who successfully negotiated the surrender of 800 German soldiers, Tournay-sur-Odon.

Violent combats in the Falaise-Chambois Pocket.

Chambois

This little village in the Orne, dominated by a 12th-century castle with a square keep, remains famous as the theatre of the last great battle for the liberation of Normandy. Chambois is located on the main road of the Dives valley. Allied hesitations meant that 100,000 German soldiers were able to regroup in this sector. The Allies surrounded them, with the Canadian and Polish armies to the north, the American armies and the 2nd French Armoured Division of General Leclerc to the south, and the British army to the west.

In the morning of August 18th, the Canadian 4th Armoured Division took Trun and Saint-Lambert. On August 19th, at 7.20 a.m., the Polish troops linked up with the 395th US Infantry Regiment, which made it possible to lock the Falaise-Chambois Pocket. The following day, the German troops tried to counter-attack, but were pushed back at the price of bloody fighting. The day after this, the German paratroopers managed to open a passage between Saint-Lambert and Coudehard: this passage became known as the "Corridor of Death". On August 21st, a deluge of fire from Spitfires, Typhoons and artillery rained down on the few square miles where the German soldiers were encircled. From the top of Mont Ormel the Poles defended this position fiercely and endlessly pounded the Germans who were trying to attack. The battle became a real carnage where men and animals perished. The Germans, who had run out of fuel, tried to flee on foot or on horseback in a gigantic scramble. Erich Braun, of the 2nd Panzerdivision, wrote later about

what the German soldiers had had to endure: *"Everywhere there was the chaos of explosions and men calling for help, the dead with their faces twisted with suffering, officers and men in a state of shock, vehicles on fire and men screaming inside, soldiers who had gone mad crying, shouting, swearing or bursting into hysterical laughter, horses whinnying in terror, still attached to their shafts and struggling on the stumps of their back legs to try to escape."* The Polish and American armies managed to rejoin the 2nd Armoured Division of General Leclerc and the 2nd British Armoured Division. This action closed up the Pocket and forced the Germans who had not managed to escape to surrender. At midday on August 21st 1944, the Battle of Normandy had been won. Over 10,000 German soldiers had been killed and 40,000 to 50,000 taken prisoner, but about the same number had escaped. The Allies also suffered heavy losses: on Mont Ormel hill, only 114 Polish soldiers out of 1,560 were still operational. The battlefields around were piled up with the bodies of men and animals and the stench was terrible because of the heat.

On August 23rd, General Eisenhower commented on the horror of this final battle: *"It was possible to walk for hundreds of yards on nothing but human remains in a state of decomposition, in heavy silence in luxuriant countryside where all life had suddenly stopped."*

The battle of the Falaise-Chambois Pocket had concluded the Battle of Normandy successfully for the Allied armies. It had also opened the way for the liberation of France, with the taking of Paris on August 24th, three days after this defeat of the armies of the Third Reich, the most bitter since the battle of Stalingrad.

Commemorative monument and keep of Chambois castle.

June 44 Museum

Mairie, Place Fulbert de Beina, 61303 L'Aigle, +33 (0)233841616
www.ville-laigle.fr
The town of L'Aigle was liberated on August 22nd 1944. Since 1953, a museum has told the story of the entire period of the Occupation, from the famous appeal of June 18th 1940 to the Liberation. Ten historical scenes show the main figures of the Second World War. An animated strategic map measuring almost 400 sq. feet tells the story of the Battle of Normandy.

June 44 Museum, L'Aigle.

Epilogue

Throughout this journey along the beaches of the Allied landings, but also inland in the countryside of Lower Normandy, each person at each moment can feel a deep emotion that is still raw. These 50 miles of French coastline are marked for ever by these first steps towards the liberation of Europe. The Second World War cemeteries attest to the heavy losses of this battle, which killed 90,000 Allied and German soldiers. Total losses (killed, missing, wounded, taken prisoner) reached more than 600,000 men (209,672 Allies and 393,689 Germans). Jean Compagnon emphasises that *"the extent of the German defeat was considerable, both in human and material terms"*. Apart from the loss of men,

the armies of the Third Reich lost 1,500 tanks, 2,000 cannons and 20,000 vehicles. Air and naval superiority tipped the balance in favour of the Allies, while the German foot-soldiers proved to be much more effective than the Allied soldiers in close combat. The landings of June 6th 1944 and the Battle of Normandy will for ever remain the decisive stages in the liberation of Europe and in the outcome of the Second World War.

Apart from these military losses, one must not forget the civilian casualties: between 15,000 and 20,000 dead, mostly as a result of the bombing. The majority of the cities had to be rebuilt: 120,000 buildings had been completely

destroyed and 270,000 damaged. Lower Normandy paid a very heavy price for its liberation, but it was the key to the liberation of Europe. In May 1944, understanding the imminence of a landing in his département, the Prefect of Calvados wrote in his monthly report: *"No one has any illusions about the ordeal of invasion awaiting our country, but it is the only solution."* Despite this ordeal, the joy of the people of Normandy on being delivered from the Nazi yoke was immense. Everyone welcomed the liberators with limitless enthusiasm.

General Dwight Eisenhower drew this conclusion after the Battle of Normandy: *"Among the reasons for our victory, one must take into account not only the successes of our troops on the battlefields but also the care and foresight involved in the preparations*

for the landings. We owe the essential factors of our success to the meticulous care taken in the preparation and organisation, such as: the degree of surprise when the landings took place, sufficient quantities of equipment and material, and the organisation which governed the exploits of our supply intendance. It is true that we had hoped that the tactical developments of the first days would allow us to seize the south and south-east region of Caen which would have meant we could build airfields... and take advantage of our armoured power, but it is no less exact that, on the scale of our overall strategy, we attained the line we had set for ourselves for D + 90 two weeks earlier than this date... But, of all the factors contributing to our victory, the most important lies undoubtedly in the qualities of the soldiers, sailors and aviators of the united nations."

Children from Normandy in the arms of GIs.

Chronology of events

1940

June 22: signing of the armistice between France and Germany

1941

June 21: opération Barbarossa
August: Newfoundland meeting between Roosevelt and Churchill
September 28: British raids on Luc-sur-Mer and Saint-Aubin-sur-Mer

1942

January 18: British raid on Saint-Laurent-sur-Mer
August 19: Operation Jubilee at Dieppe
September 13: British raid on Sainte-Honorine-des-Pertes
November 8: Landing in North Africa

1943

January 24: Casablanca Conference
February 2: German surrender in Stalingrad
May 12-25: Trident Conference in Washington
July 10: Landing in Sicily (Operation Husky)
August 17-24: Quebec Conference
December: Eisenhower leads Operation Overlord

1944

January 22: Landing at Anzio (Operation Shingle)
February: Montgomery revises Overlord
May 17: Eisenhower sets the D-Day landing for Monday June 5th
June 3: Boarding of the troops
June 6: Landings on five beaches in Lower Normandy
00:20: 6th Airborne at Pegasus Bridge
00:30: 101st dropped over Sainte-Mère-Eglise
02:30: Liberation of Ranville
82nd Airborne parachuted over the Cotentin peninsula
04:30: Liberation of Sainte-Mère-Eglise
04:45: Otway occupies Merville
06:30: Landing at Omaha Beach and Utah Beach
07:10: Rangers under Colonel Rudder at the foot of the Pointe du Hoc
07:30: Landing at Gold Beach and Sword Beach
08:00: Landing at Juno Beach
08:30: Green Berets at Riva Bella
09:30: Liberation of Bernières-sur-Mer
11:00: Liberation of Vierville-sur-Mer
13:00: Liberation of Ouistreham, Saint-Laurent-sur-Mer
19:00: Longues-sur-Mer battery neutralised
Liberation of Saint-Aubin-sur-Mer, Mauvaines, Douvres-la-Delivrande, Bény-sur-Mer, Anguerny, Tailleville, Courseulles-sur-Mer, Hermanville-sur-Mer, Graye-sur-Mer, Ver-sur-Mer, Asnelles-sur-Mer, Arromanches-les-Bains, Sainte-Marie-du-Mont, Hiesville

June 7: Liberation of Lion-sur-Mer, Luc-sur-Mer, Langrune-sur-Mer, Creully, Bayeux, Sainte-Honorine-des-Pertes, Colleville-sur-Mer, Blosville
Storming the Pointe de la Percée radar station
June 8: Liberation of Port-en-Bessin
June 9: Liberation of Grandcamp-les-Bains, Isigny-sur-Mer, Chef-du-Pont
June 12: Winston Churchill and Eisenhower arrive in Bayeux
Link-up of the American troops of the Omaha and Utah sectors
Liberation of Anfréville, Carentan
Storming of the Crisbecq battery
June 13: Liberation of Bréville
June 14: Arrival of General de Gaulle
June 15: Liberation of Quinéville
June 16: Arrival of George VI, King of England
June 18: The Cotentin peninsula is cut in two
June 19: Liberation of Montebourg, Tilly-sur-Seulles
The artificial port of Vierville-sur-Mer is destroyed by the storm
June 20: Liberation of Valognes
June 25: Operation Epsom
PLUTO pipeline at Port-en-Bessin
June 26: Liberation of Cherbourg
July 6: Taking of Carpiquet
July 7: Heavy bombardment in Caen
July 8: Assault of Mont Castre
Operation Charnwood
July 9: Liberation of La Haye-du-Puits, Ardenne Abbey and the left bank of Caen
Operation Goodwood
July 16: First Liberty ships in Cherbourg harbour

July 19: Liberation of the right bank of Caen
Operation Cobra
July 27: Liberation of Marigny and Périers
July 28: Liberation of Coutances
July 30: Liberation of Avranches
Operation Bluecoat
July 31: Liberation of Granville
August 1: Leclerc and the 2nd Armoured Division land at Saint-Martin-de-Varreville
Liberation of Saint-James
August 5: Liberation of Aunay-sur-Odon
August 7: Liberation of Vire
Operation Totalize
August 8: Liberation of Cintheaux
August 9: Liberation of Langannerie
August 12: PLUTO pipeline in Cherbourg
Liberation of Mortain
2nd Armoured Division at Alençon
August 14: Operation Tractable
August 15: Landing in Provence
August 17: Liberation of Falaise, Troarn, Robehomme, Condé-sur-Noireau
August 19: Taking of Mont Ormel
August 21: End of the Chambois battle
August 22: Liberation of L'Aigle
August 23: Liberation of Lisieux
August 25: Liberation of Paris
September 12: Liberation of Le Havre and end of the Battle of Normandy
November 2: Cherbourg is the world's leading port

1945

May 8: Germany signs unconditional surrender.

Second World War cemeteries

As soon as the fighting began it claimed victims, the numbers rising each day. British Lieutenant Dan Brotheridge was the first to be killed after the landing at Pegasus Bridge. As the battles raged on, the dead were left on the ground; it was only during moments of calm that they could be buried where they had fallen. The Americans built their first cemetery on the coast at the foot of the cliffs between Saint-Laurent-sur-Mer and Vierville-sur-Mer. Two temporary cemeteries were also set up near Sainte-Mère-Eglise. In the urgency of the situation, Allied and German bodies were buried together, such as in La Cambe; the American bodies were later exhumed and sent to Colleville-sur-Mer, while the German bodies remained in La Cambe. Some 100,000 soldiers – around 40,000 Allies and 60,000 Germans – are buried in Lower Normandy, but the majority (mainly Americans) were sent back to their home countries. The British remain buried where they fell, however, according to British custom. Their cemeteries also contain the bodies of soldiers from other countries, including Germans. The cemeteries were organised at the end of the 1940s and throughout the 1950s. The cemetery in Colleville-sur-Mer, inaugurated on July 18th 1956, is located on a 172-acre site that has been granted in perpetuity to the United States. The German cemetery in La Cambe was inaugurated on 21st September 1961. The cemetery in Tourgéville is the only instance of a First World War cemetery being reused to bury the victims of the Second World War. Some soldiers' graves can also be found in civilian cemeteries. The bodies of British soldiers found over the years have been buried in the cemetery in Saint-Charles-de-Percy, while those of German soldiers have been buried in the cemetery in La Cambe; this was the case of Michael Wittmann, whose body was only found in 1982.

The various countries are responsible for the upkeep of their cemeteries: the American Battle Monuments Commission, the German War Graves Commission and the Commonwealth War Graves Commission. The Polish cemetery in Langannerie is managed by the War Graves Department attached to the French Secretariat for Defence with responsibility for War Veterans. These agencies are responsible for the organisation and administration of these cemeteries and also for the upkeep of the graves.

American cemeteries:
Colleville-sur-Mer: 9,387 graves including 307 unknown and 4 women. 1,557 names are inscribed in the Garden of the Missing.
Saint-James: 4,410 graves. The names of 498 of the missing are inscribed on a wall.

British cemeteries:
Banneville-la-Campagne: 2,175 including 11 Canadians, 5 Australians, 2 New Zealanders, 5 Polish and 2 unknown.
Bayeux: 4,648 including 181 Canadians, 17 Australians, 8 New Zealanders, 1 South African, 25

Polish, 3 French, 2 Czechs, 2 Italians, 7 Russians and 466 Germans. It includes a Memorial bearing the name of 2,092 soldiers, including 270 Canadians and 1 South African, who have no grave.
Brouay: 377 including 2 Canadians.
Cambes-en-Plaine: 224.
Chouain, known as Jerusalem: 47 including 1 Czech.
Douvres-la-Délivrande: 1,123 including 1 Polish, 11 Canadians, 3 Australians, 180 Germans and 1 unknown.
Fontenay-le-Pesnel: 520 including 4 Canadians and 59 Germans.
Hermanville-sur-Mer: 1,005 including 13 Canadians, 3 Australians and 2 French.
Hottot-les-Bagues: 1,137 including 34 Canadians, 3 Australians, 2 New Zealanders, 1 South African and 132 Germans.
Ranville: 2,562 including 76 Canadians, 1 Australian, 1 Belgian, 322 Germans and 1 unknown.
Ryes-Bazenville: 979 including 21 Canadians, 1 Australian, 1 Polish and 326 Germans.
Saint-Charles-de-Percy: 789 including 3 Canadians.
Saint-Désir-de-Lisieux: 598 including 16 Canadians, 6 Australians, 1 New Zealander, 5 South Africans and 1 American.
Saint-Manvieu-Norrey: 2,183 including 3 Canadians, 1 Australian and 356 Germans.
Secqueville-en-Bessin: 117 including 18 Germans and 1 unknown.
Tilly-sur-Seulles: 1,222 including 2 New Zealanders, 1 Canadian, 1 Australian and 223 Germans.
Tourgéville: 105 including 13 British, 90 Germans and 2 civilians.

Civilian cemeteries:
Bénouville: 23.
Hérouvillette: 27.
Ranville: 47.

French cemeteries:
Nécropole de **Gateys**: 19 soldiers from the 2nd Armoured Division.
Montjoie Saint-Martin: monument built in 1999 in honour of 8 Moroccan soldiers from the 2nd Armoured Division.

Canadian cemeteries:
Bény-sur-Mer – Reviers: 2,049 including 4 British and 1 French.
Cintheaux: 2,958 including 87 unknown, 80 British, 4 Australians, 1 New Zealander and 1 French.

Polish cemetery:
Grainville-Langannerie: 696. These are mostly the graves of soldiers from the 1st Armoured Division of General Maczek.

German cemeteries:
Huisnes-sur-Mer: 11,956. The cemetery is composed of 68 crypts, each containing 180 bodies.
La Cambe: 21,400 including a tumulus with 296 unknown.
Marigny – La-Chapelle-en-Juger: 11,169.
Orglandes: 10,152.
Saint-Désir-de-Lisieux: 3,735. The cemetery contains thin beds of irises, each planted at the foot of a red sandstone cross bearing the name of 4 soldiers.

There is a sixth German cemetery in Upper Normandy, in **Champigny-la-Futelaie**: 19,954 graves.

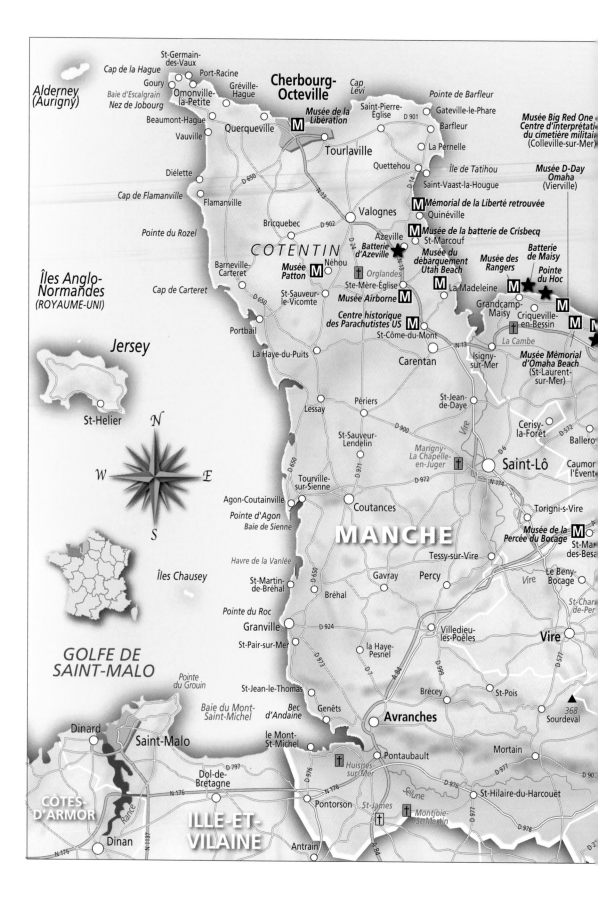

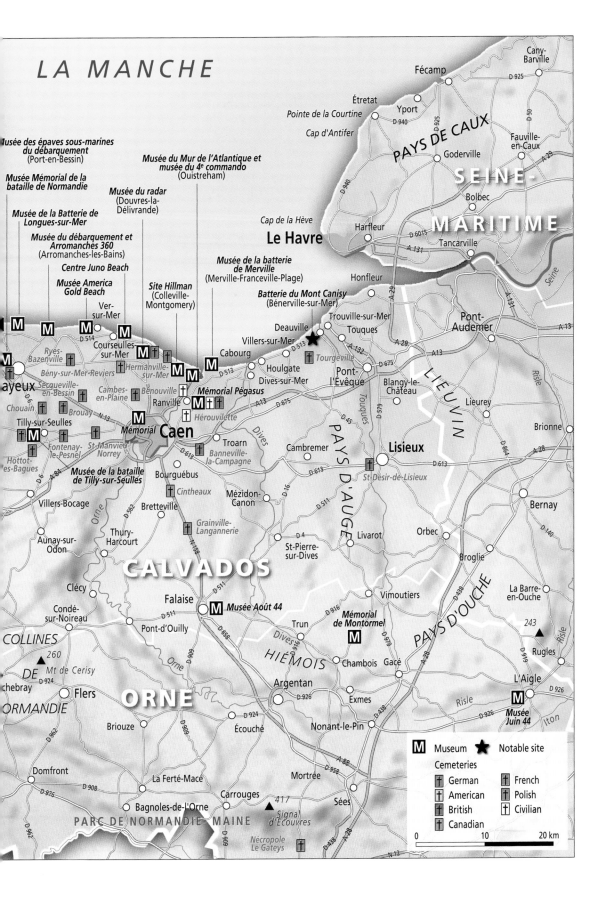

LA MANCHE

Cany-Barville

Fécamp

Étretat
Yport
Pointe de la Courtine
D 940
Cap d'Antifer

PAYS DE CAUX

Goderville

Fauville-en-Caux
A 29

SEINE-

Bolbec

MARITIME

Harfleur
D 6015
Tancarville

Cap de la Hève

Le Havre
A 131

Seine

A 131

Musée des épaves sous-marines
du débarquement
(Port-en-Bessin)

Musée du Mur de l'Atlantique et
musée du 4e commando
(Ouistreham)

Musée Mémorial de la
bataille de Normandie

Musée du radar
(Douvres-la-
Délivrande)

Musée de la Batterie de
Longues-sur-Mer

Musée du débarquement et
Arromanches 360
(Arromanches-les-Bains)

Centre Juno Beach

Musée America
Gold Beach

Ver-
sur-Mer

Site Hillman
(Colleville-
Montgomery)

Musée de la batterie
de Merville
(Merville-Franceville-Plage)

Honfleur

Batterie du Mont Canisy
(Bénerville-sur-Mer)

Trouville-sur-Mer
Touques

Pont-
Audemer

A 13

Deauville
Villers-sur-Mer
A 132
A 29
A 13

LIEUVIN

Risle

M **M** **M** **M**
D 514
Courseulles-
sur-Mer

Cabourg
D 513
Tourgéville

Pont-
l'Évêque
D 675

Blangy-le-
Château

Lieurey

Brionne

M
ayeux

Ryes-
Bazenville
Bény-sur-Mer-Reviers
Hermanville-
sur-Mer

Houlgate
Dives-sur-Mer
D 513

Toques
D 579
D 675

D 864
A 28

Sequeville-
en-Bessin
Cambes-
en-Plaine
Bénouville
Mémorial Pégasus

A 13

St-Désir-de-Lisieux

Lisieux
D 613

Chouain
Brouay
N 13
Ranville
M
Hérouvillette

D 45

PAYS D'AUGE

Tilly-sur-Seulles
M
Mémorial **Caen**

Troarn
Banneville-
Ja-Campagne
Dives

Cambremer
D 613

Bernay

Fontenay-
le-Pesnel
St-Manvieu-
Norrey
D 613

Bourguébus

D 16

Livarot

Orbec

Hottot-
es-Bagues

Musée de la bataille
de Tilly-sur-Seulles

Cintheaux

Mézidon-
Canon
D 511

Broglie

Villers-Bocage

Orne
D 562
Bretteville

Grainville-
Langannerie
N 158

D 4
St-Pierre-
sur-Dives

Vimoutiers
D 438
La Barre-
en-Ouche

Aunay-sur-
Odon

Thury-
Harcourt

Risle
243
Rugles

Clécy

Falaise
M Musée Août 44
D 511

Mémorial
de Montormel
M

PAYS D'OUCHE

COLLINES

Condé-
sur-Noireau

Pont-d'Ouilly

D 916

Trun

Dives
D 916

Chambois
Gacé

D 919

L'Aigle
D 926

DE
Mt de Cerisy
D 924

260

HIÉMOIS

Orne
D 909

M
Musée
Juin 44
Iton

chebray
Flers

ORNE

Argentan
D 926

Exmes
D 438
A 28
Risle
D 926

ORMANDIE

Briouze

Écouché

Nonant-le-Pin

Domfront

La Ferté-Macé
D 908

Mortrée
D 958

Carrouges
417

Bagnoles-de-l'Orne
D 962

Signal
d'Écouvres

Sées
D 438
A 28

PARC DE NORMANDIE-MAINE
606

N 12

Nécropole
Le Gateys

M Museum	⭐ Notable site	
Cemeteries		
✝ German	✝ French	
✝ American	✝ Polish	
✝ British	✝ Civilian	
✝ Canadian		

0   10   20 km

The Historical Area of the Battle of Normandy

Calvados Tourist Board
Place du Canada, 14000 Caen
Tel.: + 33 (0)2 31 27 90 30
Fax: + 33 (0)02 31 27 90 35
E-mail: calvatour@mail.cpod.fr

Manche Tourist Board
Maison du Département,
50008 Saint-Lô Cedex
Tel.: + 33 (0)2 33 05 98 70
Fax: + 33 (0)2 33 56 07 03

Orne Tourist Board
88 rue de Saint-Blaise
BP 50, 61002 Alençon Cedex
Tel.: +33 (0)2 33 28 88 71
Fax: + 33 (0)2 33 29 81 60
E-mail: orne.tourisme@wanadoo.fr

Normandy Tourist Board
Le Doyenné
14 rue Charles-Corbeau
27000 Evreux
Tel.: + 33 (0)2 32 33 94 00
Fax: + 33 (0)2 32 31 19 04
E-mail: normandy@imaginet.fr
Internet: www.normandy-tourism.fr

Bibliography

Bataille de Normandie, Guides Gallimard, 1994.
BARBE Dominique,
    Charnwood, la bataille de Buron-Saint-Contest,
    Editions Corlet, 1994.
BEEVOR Anthony,
    D-Day et la bataille de Normandie,
    Editions Calman-Lévy, 2008.
BOLLORE Gwenn-Aël,
    *J'ai débarqué le 6 juin 1944-Commando de la France
    libre*, Editions Le Cherche Midi, 2004.
BOUSQUET Patrick and HECTOR Régis,
    Les Héros du Jour J, Editions OREP, 2006.
CARELL Paul,
    *Ils arrivent ! La bataille de Normandie vue du côté
    allemand*, Editions Robert Laffont, 1962.
COMPAGNON Jean,
    Les Plages du débarquement, Editions Ouest-France,
    1979.

COQUART Elizabeth and HUET Philippe,
    Le jour le plus fou-6 juin 1944,
    Editions Albin Michel, 1994.
DESQUESNES Rémy,
    Le Mur de l'Atlantique-Normandie 1944,
    Editions OREP.
DESQUESNES Rémy,
    *Le Mur de l'Atlantique du Mont-Saint-Michel
    au Tréport*, Editions Ouest-France, 2004.
DESQUESNES Rémy,
    *Normandie 44-Le débarquement et la bataille
    de Normandie*, Editions Ouest-France, 2009.
FOURNIER Gérard and HEINTZ André,
    Opération Aquatint, Editions OREP, 2006.
GOCKEL Franz,
    *La Porte de l'enfer-Omaha Beach
    6 juin 1944*, Editions Hirle, 2004.

GOSSET André and LECOMTE Paul,
Caen pendant la bataille, Caen, 1946.

GUENO Jean-Pierre and PECNARD Jérôme,
Paroles du Jour J-Carnets du débarquement-Eté 44,
Editions Les Arènes, 2004.

HENRY Jacques,
*La Normandie en flammes, Normands et Canadiens
dans la bataille de 1944*, Editions Corlet, 1984.

HERVEZ-BAUDIN Pascal,
*Opération Gooseberry, 7-10 juin-Les premiers ports
artificiels*, Editions Inédits et Introuvables, 2006.

INGOUF-KNOCKER Paul,
Juin 40-44 en Cotentin, objectif(s) Cherbourg,
Editions Inédits et Introuvables, 2004.

JACQUET Stéphane,
La Bataille de Tilly sur Seulles, Editions Heimdal,
2009.

JUILLARD Jean,
Le Plan Violet PTT, Editions Lavauzelle, 2009.

KEMP Anthony,
6 juin 1944, Débarquement en Normandie,
Editions Gallimard, 1994.

KIEFFER Philippe,
Les Bérets verts français du 6 juin 1944,
Editions France-Empire, 2004.

LE CACHEUX Geneviève and QUELLIEN Jean,
*Dictionnaire de la libération du nord-ouest
de la France*, Editions Corlet, 1994.

LECŒUR Maurice,
Sainte-Mère-Eglise, le village du Jour le plus long,
Editions Lieu Commun, 1994.

LECOUTURIER Yves,
Les Plages du débarquement, Collection Itinéraires
de découvertes, Editions Ouest-France, 1999.

LE PENVEN Eris and SIMONNET Stéphane,
N° 4 Commando, Editions Heimdal, 2004.

LEROUVILLOIS Robert,
Et la liberté vint de Cherbourg,
Editions Corlet, 1991.

LEROUVILLOIS Robert,
*Cherbourg, port de la liberté dans la bataille
de Normandie*, Editions Isoète, 2009.

L'Histoire n° 287, May 2004.

L'Ouest en guerre, newspaper *Ouest-France*, 2004.

MACKEE Alexander,
La Bataille de Caen, Presses de la Cité, 1965.

MAN John,
*Atlas du débarquement et de la bataille
de Normandie 6 juin-24 août 1944*,
Editions Autrement, 1994.

MOREAU Jean-Bernard,
Le Débarquement et la bataille de Normandie,
Editions Le Mémorial de Caen, 2004.

PERRAULT Gilles,
Le secret du Jour J, Editions Fayard, 2004.

PINEL Michel,
La guerre des haies et la bataille de La Haye-du-Puits,
Editions Inédits et Introuvables, 2009.

POIRIER Joseph,
La Bataille de Caen, Caron, 1945.

QUELLIEN Jean,
La Normandie au cœur de la guerre,
Editions Ouest-France/Mémorial, 1992.

QUELLIEN Jean,
90 jours qui ont changé le monde,
newspaper *Ouest-France* from June 2nd to August
29th 2004.

RUFFIN Raymond,
La Résistance dans l'opération Overlord,
Editions France-Empire, 2004.

RUPPERTHAL Roland G.,
*The European Theater of Operations: Logistical
Support of the Armies*,
Vol. 1 May 1941-Sept.1944, Washington Office of the
Chief of Military History, 1953.

Voix de vétérans, Centre Juno Beach, 2009.

WIEVORKA Olivier,
*Histoire du débarquement en Normandie
des origines à Paris*, Editions Le Seuil, 2007.

Table of contents

All the historical photographs come from the archives of the
Caen Memorial.

Editors: Henri Bancaud and Matthieu Biberon
Editorial coordination: Caroline Brou
Page layout: Brigitte Racine
Maps: Patrick Mérienne
Photo-engraving: graph&ti, Cesson-Sévigné (35)
Printing: Pollina à Luçon (85) - L56546E

© 2011, Éditions Ouest-France
Édilarge SA, Rennes
ISBN 978-2-7373-5333-8
Publisher number: 6437.01.4,5.03.11
Legal deposit: March 2011
Printed in France
Find us at www.editionsouestfrance.fr